SPECTRUM®

Test Prep

Grade 5

Published by Spectrum®
an imprint of Carson-Dellosa Publishing LLC
Greensboro, NC

Spectrum®
An imprint of Carson-Dellosa Publishing LLC
P.O. Box 35665
Greensboro, NC 27425 USA

ISBN 978-0-7696-8625-7

11-333127784

Table of Contents

Social Studies

Science

What's Inside?

This workbook is designed to help you and your fifth grader understand what he or she will be expected to know on standardized tests.

Practice Pages

The workbook is divided into four sections: English Language Arts, Mathematics, Social Studies, and Science. The practice activities in this workbook provide students with practice in each of these areas. Each section has practice activities that have questions similar to those that will appear on the standardized tests. Students should use a pencil to fill in the correct answers and to complete any writing on these activities.

National Standards

Before each practice section is a list of the national standards covered by that section. These standards list the knowledge and skills that students are expected to master at each grade level. The shaded *What it means* sections will help to explain any information in the standards that might be unfamiliar.

Mini-Tests and Final Tests

When your student finishes the practice pages for specific standards, your student can move on to a mini-test that covers the material presented on those practice activities. After an entire set of standards and accompanying practice pages are completed, your student should take the final tests, which incorporate materials from all the practice pages in that section.

Final Test Answer Sheet

The final tests have a separate answer sheet that mimics the style of the answer sheets the students will use on the standardized tests. The answer sheets appear at the end of each final test.

How Am I Doing?

The *How Am I Doing?* pages are designed to help students identify areas where they are proficient and areas where they still need more practice. They will pinpoint areas where more work is needed, as well as areas where your student excels. Students can keep track of each of their mini-test scores on these pages.

Answer Key

Answers to all the practice pages, mini-tests, and final tests are listed by page number and appear at the end of the book.

To find a complete listing of the national standards in each subject area, you can access the following Web sites:

The National Council of Teachers of English: www.ncte.org
National Council of Teachers of Mathematics: www.nctm.org/standards
National Council for the Social Studies: www.ncss.org/standards
National Science Teachers Association: www.nsta.org/standards

English Language Arts Standards

Standard 1 *(See pages 9–12.)*
Students read a wide range of print and nonprint texts to build an understanding of texts, of themselves, and of the cultures of the United States and the world; to acquire new information; to respond to the needs and demands of society and the workplace; and for personal fulfillment. Among these texts are fiction and nonfiction, classic and contemporary works.

Standard 2 *(See pages 11–14.)*
Students read a wide range of literature from many periods in many genres to build an understanding of the many dimensions (e.g., philosophical, ethical, aesthetic) of human experience.

Standard 3 *(See pages 15–16.)*
Students apply a wide range of strategies to comprehend, interpret, evaluate, and appreciate texts. They draw on their prior experience, their interactions with other readers and writers, their knowledge of word meaning and of other texts, their word identification strategies, and their understanding of textual features (e.g., sound-letter correspondence, sentence structure, context, graphics).

Standard 4 *(See pages 18–21.)*
Students adjust their use of spoken, written, and visual language (e.g., conventions, style, vocabulary) to communicate effectively with a variety of audiences and for different purposes.

Standard 5 *(See pages 22–24.)*
Students employ a wide range of strategies as they write and use different writing process elements appropriately to communicate with different audiences for a variety of purposes.

Standard 6 *(See pages 25–28.)*
Students apply knowledge of language structure, language conventions (e.g., spelling and punctuation), media techniques, figurative language, and genre to create, critique, and discuss print and nonprint texts.

Standard 7 *(See page 30.)*
Students conduct research on issues and interests by generating ideas and questions, and by posing problems. They gather, evaluate, and synthesize data from a variety of sources (e.g., print and nonprint texts, artifacts, people) to communicate their discoveries in ways that suit their purpose and audience.

Standard 8 *(See pages 31–32.)*
Students use a variety of technological and informational resources (e.g., libraries, databases, computer networks, video) to gather and synthesize information and to create and communicate knowledge.

Standard 9 *(See page 34.)*
Students develop an understanding of and respect for diversity in language use, patterns, and dialects across cultures, ethnic groups, geographic regions, and social roles.

Standard 10
Students whose first language is not English make use of their first language to develop competency in the English language arts and to develop understanding of content across the curriculum.

English Language Arts Standards

Standard 11 *(See page 35.)*
Students participate as knowledgeable, reflective, creative, and critical members of a variety of literacy communities.

Standard 12 *(See page 36.)*
Students use spoken, written, and visual language to accomplish their own purposes (e.g., for learning, enjoyment, persuasion, and the exchange of information).

Name _____ Date _____

1.0

Differences Between Fiction and Nonfiction
Reading and Comprehension

DIRECTIONS: Read the passages. Then, in each of the lists, circle the characteristics that you think are true about each passage.

Hibernation

Have you ever wondered why some animals hibernate? Hibernation is when animals sleep through the winter. Animals get their warmth and energy from food. Some animals cannot find enough food in the winter, so they must eat large amounts of food in the fall. Their bodies store this food as fat. Then, in winter, they hibernate and their bodies live on the stored fat. Since their bodies need much less food during hibernation, they can stay alive without eating new food during the winter. Some animals that hibernate are bats, chipmunks, bears, snakes, and turtles.

Waterland

"Hurray!" cried Meghan. "Today is the day we're going to Waterland!" It was a hot July day, and Meghan's mom was taking her and her new friend Jake.

Just then, Meghan's mom came out of her bedroom. She did not look very happy. "What's the matter, Mom? Are you afraid to get wet?" Meghan teased.

Mrs. Millett told the kids that she wasn't felling well. She was too tired to drive to the water park.

Meghan and Jake were disappointed. "My mom has chronic fatigue syndrome," Meghan explained. "Her illness makes her really tired. She's still a great mom."

"Thank you, dear," said Mrs. Millett. "I'm too tired to drive, but I have an idea. You can make your own Waterland, and I'll rest in the lawn chair."

Meghan and Jake set up three different sprinklers. They dragged the play slide over to the wading pool and aimed the sprinkler on the slide. Meghan and Jake got soaking wet and played all day.

"Thank you for being so understanding," Meghan's mom said. "Now, I feel better, but I'm really hot! There's only one cure for that." She stood under the sprinkler with all her clothes on. She was drenched from head to toe.

Meghan laughed and said, "Now you have chronic wet syndrome." Mrs. Millett rewarded her daughter with a big, wet hug.

Hibernation	Waterland
Includes facts	Includes facts
Made up or fantasized	Made up or fantasized
Main purpose is to inform	Main purpose is to inform
Main purpose is to entertain	Main purpose is to entertain
Organized into setting, characters, problem, goal, events, and resolution	Organized into setting, characters, problem, goal, events, and resolution
Organized according to the purpose the authors wish to achieve (steps to achieve a goal; explain why something happens; attempt to make an argument; etc.)	Organized according to the purpose the authors wish to achieve (steps to achieve a goal; explain why something happens; attempt to make an argument; etc.)

Name _____ Date _____

Applying Appropriate Reading Strategies
Reading and Comprehension

DIRECTIONS: Read the passages and answer the questions that follow.

A

Wasps build new nests every year. The potter wasp creates a mud "jar" nest for each of its eggs. The wasp then stings caterpillars to paralyze them and places them in the jar nests. The nests are sealed, and the caterpillars are used as food for the developing wasps.

B

Laura Ingalls Wilder wrote a series of nine children's books about her life as a pioneer. The first book was titled *Little House in the Big Woods.* Laura's books have been praised for their portrayals of life on the American frontier.

C

Ice hockey originated in the mid-1800s when British troops played games of field hockey on the frozen lakes and ponds of Canada's provinces of Ontario and Nova Scotia. It became Canada's national sport by the early 1900s. Since then, the sport has become popular in European countries such as Russia and Sweden, as well as in the United States.

D

One day, just as the leaves were beginning to change color, Rip Van Winkle walked through the woods and up the mountains. By early afternoon, he found himself on one of the highest points of the Catskill Mountains. By late afternoon, Rip was tired and panting, so he found a spot with a beautiful view where he could lie down and rest. Through an opening in the trees, Rip could see miles and miles of lower country and rich woodland. In the distance, he could view the mighty Hudson River. It was moving calmly along its course, showing reflections of the soft white clouds in the sky.

E

Chevy 1984 Cavalier. Has all 4 tires. Runs. May need work. You must haul it away yourself. $500 or best offer. Call Clutch at 555-4343.

F

As she walked along the sandy shore with delight at nature's wonders, she saw starfish, whitecaps, conch shells, and more. She knew that she would never fly free like the tissue-paper seagulls above or swim with the dolphins she loved.

1. **Which of the passages are nonfiction?**

_____

_____

2. **Which passage requires you to pay particular attention to figurative language?**

_____

_____

3. **Which passage would you be more likely to read with an eye to literal truth—passage B or passage D?**

_____

_____

4. **Which passage could you more easily illustrate on a time line—passage C or passage E?**

_____

_____

5. **Which passage requires you to pay particular attention to a sequence of events—passage A or passage B?**

_____

_____

Name _____   Date _____

Different Forms of Literature
Reading and Comprehension

DIRECTIONS: Read the passage below, and answer questions 1–4.

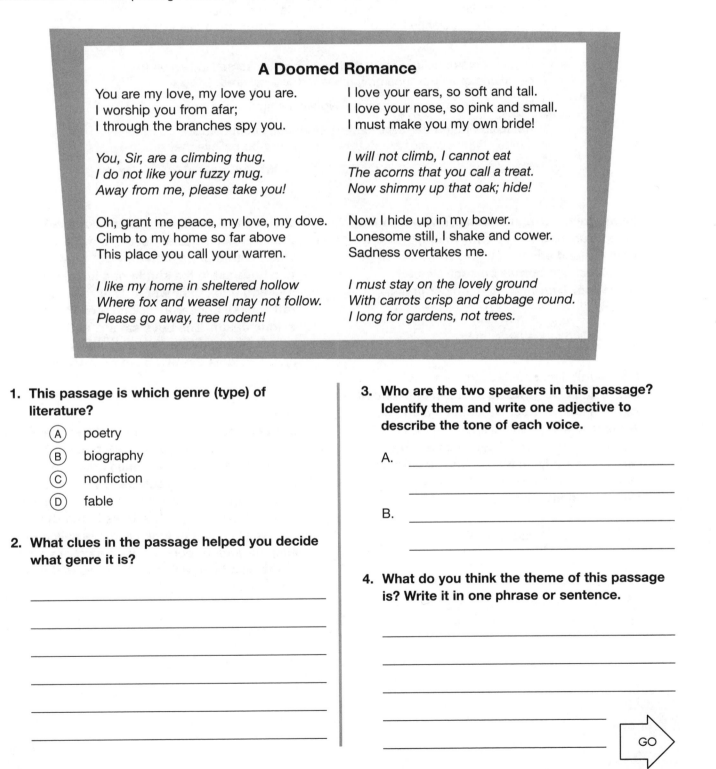

A Doomed Romance

You are my love, my love you are.
I worship you from afar;
I through the branches spy you.

You, Sir, are a climbing thug.
I do not like your fuzzy mug.
Away from me, please take you!

Oh, grant me peace, my love, my dove.
Climb to my home so far above
This place you call your warren.

I like my home in sheltered hollow
Where fox and weasel may not follow.
Please go away, tree rodent!

I love your ears, so soft and tall.
I love your nose, so pink and small.
I must make you my own bride!

I will not climb, I cannot eat
The acorns that you call a treat.
Now shimmy up that oak; hide!

Now I hide up in my bower.
Lonesome still, I shake and cower.
Sadness overtakes me.

I must stay on the lovely ground
With carrots crisp and cabbage round.
I long for gardens, not trees.

1. **This passage is which genre (type) of literature?**

   Ⓐ poetry

   Ⓑ biography

   Ⓒ nonfiction

   Ⓓ fable

2. **What clues in the passage helped you decide what genre it is?**

   _____

   _____

   _____

   _____

   _____

3. **Who are the two speakers in this passage? Identify them and write one adjective to describe the tone of each voice.**

   A. _____

   _____

   B. _____

   _____

4. **What do you think the theme of this passage is? Write it in one phrase or sentence.**

   _____

   _____

   _____

   _____

GO ⟶

Name _____ Date _____

DIRECTIONS: Read each story below and write the kind of story it is on the line.

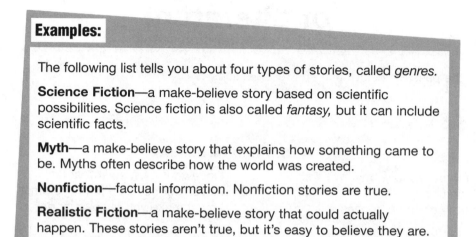

Examples:

The following list tells you about four types of stories, called *genres*.

Science Fiction—a make-believe story based on scientific possibilities. Science fiction is also called *fantasy,* but it can include scientific facts.

Myth—a make-believe story that explains how something came to be. Myths often describe how the world was created.

Nonfiction—factual information. Nonfiction stories are true.

Realistic Fiction—a make-believe story that could actually happen. These stories aren't true, but it's easy to believe they are.

5. Juniper trees grow in Arizona. Tiny fairies live in their trunks. During the full moon, the fairies come out and dance at night. While dancing, they place blue berries on each tree for decoration. That's how the juniper gets its berries.

_____

6. "It's a bird!" Tim shouted. "It's a plane!" Connie said. But it was a spaceship! It landed next to a juniper tree. Little green men got off the spaceship. They clipped off several branches of the tree. "They're collecting tree samples to study on Mars," Connie whispered. They watched, amazed, as the spaceship disappeared into the sky.

_____

7. Jason and Patrick went for a hike. Because they were in the high desert, they carried water with them. When they got tired, the two boys sat in the shade of a juniper tree to rest and drink their water. That's when the rattlesnake appeared. "Don't move!" Patrick said to Jason. The boys sat still until the snake moved away. "What an adventure!" Jason said as the two boys returned home.

_____

8. Juniper trees are small, gnarly trees that grow in many parts of the world. Members of the evergreen family, they remain green year round. Juniper trees can be easily identified by their tiny blue or red berries. There are 13 different kinds of juniper trees in the United States. One kind of juniper tree is called the *alligator juniper* because its bark looks similar to the skin of an alligator. It grows in the Southwest.

_____

Name _____   Date _____

Reading a Wide Range of Nonfiction
Reading and Comprehension

DIRECTIONS: The passages below are either from a newspaper, an instruction manual, a textbook, or a biography. Read the passages, then identify the source of each.

1. The best way to understand the food web is to study a model of it. Refer to Figure 2.3 to see a model of a food web in a deciduous forest. Recall that in Chapter 1 we identified animals as either herbivores, carnivores, or omnivores. Which animals in Figure 2.3 could best be described as herbivores?

   _____

2. LONDON, England— Buckingham Palace announced today that Queen Elizabeth will make a short visit to the United States early next week to attend the annual Westhampton Flower Show in Westhampton, Connecticut. The Queen has made several trips to the flower show, often accompanied by other members of the royal family. Last year the prize-winning rose at the show was named in honor of the Queen.

   _____

3. Wolfgang Amadeus Mozart was born on January 27,1756, in Austria. When he was just three years old, he learned to play the harpsichord. He was composing music by the time he was five years old. At the age of six, he was invited to perform for the Empress of Austria. Mozart astonished people with his musical ability. He was called a child genius.

   _____

4. Step 1: Find Pieces A, B, and C and Main Frame 1.
   Step 2: Insert Piece A into the square slot on Piece B.
   Step 3: Insert Piece C into the round slot on Piece B.
   Step 4: Snap the assembled ABC assembly into Main Frame 1.

   _____

DIRECTIONS: Based on the titles below, identify the form of nonfiction of each.

5. *Sports Weekly*
   - (A) magazine
   - (B) textbook
   - (C) essay
   - (D) reference book

6. *Dinner in Under an Hour*
   - (F) newspaper
   - (G) cookbook
   - (H) science journal
   - (J) computer manual

English Language Arts

| 2.0 |

Comparing Different Styles and Points of View
Reading and Comprehension

DIRECTIONS: Read the selections that follow, then answer the questions.

February 10

I did it! Well, I didn't win first place, but I came in second. I'm really proud of that.

At first, I was scared when I looked out and saw all those people in the audience. I was afraid I'd forget everything. But then I told myself, "You studied hard. You know all those words. Come on, you can do it!"

My first word was *indicate:* i-n-d-i-c-a-t-e. It was easy. Then, I knew I could do the rest of them, too. The only word that really stumped me was *cannibal.* I spelled it c-a-n-n-i-b-l-e—oops. Rebecca spelled it right, along with her last word: *hydraulics.*

Oh well. I won a dictionary and had my picture taken for the newspaper. When I came home, my family had a party to celebrate! Tomorrow, I start studying for next year's contest.

Local Boy Finishes Second in Regional Spelling Bee

February 10—Ben Hanson, age 10, of Park Creek, finished second in the Regional Spelling Bee sponsored by the Literacy Society. He spelled eight words correctly, finally stumbling over the word *cannibal.* Hanson won a new dictionary for his efforts.

Rebecca Cohen, from Detroit, Michigan, won first prize for spelling the word *hydraulics.* She will receive a $100 savings bond and go on to the National Spelling Bee held in Washington, D.C., next month.

---

1. **Identify the form of nonfiction of each of the two passages.**

   _____

   _____

   _____

2. **Who wrote the first passage? Where did the second passage appear?**

   _____

   _____

   _____

3. **Name three similarities between the passages.**

   _____

   _____

   _____

4. **Name three differences between the passages.**

   _____

   _____

   _____

English Language Arts

| 3.0 |

Identifying
Unknown Words
Reading and Comprehension

DIRECTIONS: Read the passage. Then, define the terms that follow using information in the passage.

Budget

Always running out of money? Have no idea where your money goes? Saving for a special trip, activity, or object? If you answered *yes* to any of these questions, it is time to plan a budget and stick to it. Budgets have a bad rap as being too restrictive or too hard to follow. In reality, a budget can be very simple, and understanding how to use one can help you save for special things. There are three easy steps to follow.

The first step in building a livable budget is to record your spending habits. Look at your expenditures. Do you buy your lunch? Do you buy a soft drink or even water from a machine? You may discover you spend money foolishly. Buying a candy bar for $0.50 every day may seem insignificant, but by the end of the month, it adds up to $15.00. Instead, put a snack in your backpack.

The next step is determining your debits and credits. Look at what money comes in and what goes out. If you have determined your spending habits, you know what your debits are. Credits might be harder to determine if you do not have a job. Determine all the ways you get money. For example, count the dollars you earn or money given to you as presents. How much each week do you have available to spend? What are your sources of income? If you do not have a regular source of income, you need to find ways to make money. Do you have an allowance? Can you negotiate with your parents to raise your allowance? Offer to do more chores or special jobs that will increase your income. Check out the neighborhood. Lawn work and babysitting are two jobs that you might like. Remember, your debits should not be more than your credits.

The last step is determining your cash flow and savings goals. How much money do you have available each week to spend? You might budget a small cash flow for yourself because you want to save for a new pair of skis, which means you might earn $10.00 a week but only allow yourself to spend $3.00. Look at three important categories. How much money do you wish to save? How much money do you need for essentials? How much money do you want for frivolous activities? Determining the balance between savings goals and cash flow is an important decision for any budget.

1. expenditures

_____

_____

2. debit

_____

_____

3. credit

_____

_____

4. cash flow

_____

_____

English Language Arts

| 3.0 |

Using Context Clues
Reading and Comprehension

DIRECTIONS: Read the paragraph. Find the word that best completes each numbered blank below.

Example:

The United States Capitol is well known for its ___(A)___, or round room. The room has a large dome. A bronze Statue of Freedom ___(B)___ on top of the dome.

A.
- (A) parlor
- (B) library
- (C) rotunda
- (D) media center

Answer: (C)

B.
- (F) stands
- (G) centered
- (H) flies
- (J) bends

Answer: (F)

Clue — Look carefully at each answer. Choose the word that sounds best in the sentence.

The Montgolfier brothers ___(1)___ the hot-air balloon in 1783. However, they ___(2)___ never guessed how high or how far one of these balloons could go. In the brothers' first ___(3)___, they used a huge bag made of paper and ___(4)___. They held its open end over a ___(5)___. The bag filled with smoke and hot air. Then, it rose into the air and ___(6)___ for a mile and a half.

1.
- (A) discovered
- (B) invented
- (C) explored
- (D) arranged

2.
- (F) probably
- (G) randomly
- (H) rarely
- (J) frequently

3.
- (A) grade
- (B) demonstration
- (C) hope
- (D) suggestion

4.
- (F) steel
- (G) bricks
- (H) mortar
- (J) fabric

5.
- (A) pool
- (B) puddle
- (C) fire
- (D) engine

6.
- (F) dropped
- (G) recorded
- (H) sank
- (J) floated

STOP

English Language Arts

1.0–3.0

For pages 9–16

DIRECTIONS: Identify the genre of each passage.

1. The children awoke to a happy sight. While they slept, the world had turned white. Their mother peered into their room and said, "No school today. Go back to bed!"
   - (A) biography
   - (B) nonfiction
   - (C) fiction
   - (D) fable

2. Police officers carry equipment that helps them to protect themselves and other people. They carry guns, nightsticks, flashlights, and handcuffs on their belts. Some wear bullet-proof vests. They also carry two-way radios so they can call other officers for assistance.
   - (F) poetry
   - (G) nonfiction
   - (H) myth
   - (J) biography

3. TINYTOWN, Indiana—The Tinytown Lady Viking basketball team grabbed its seventh victory of the season on Friday night as the team defeated the Eastside Royals 58–46.
   - (A) biography
   - (B) instruction manual
   - (C) newspaper
   - (D) textbook

4. *Antique Monthly*
   - (F) biography
   - (G) cookbook
   - (H) textbook
   - (J) magazine

DIRECTIONS: Read the paragraph. Find the word that fits best in each numbered blank.

   People who travel or cross the Amazon and Orinoco Rivers of South America are careful never to ____(5)____ a foot or hand from the side of their boat. Just below the surface of these mighty waters ____(6)____ a small fish feared throughout the ____(7)____. That fish is the flesh-eating piranha. Although smaller fish make up most of its diet, the piranha will ____(8)____ both humans and other animals.

5. (A) lift
   - (B) dangle
   - (C) withdraw
   - (D) brush

6. (F) lurks
   - (G) nests
   - (H) plays
   - (J) boasts

7. (A) universe
   - (B) town
   - (C) continent
   - (D) village

8. (F) befriend
   - (G) bully
   - (H) attack
   - (J) analyze

English Language Arts

4.0

Acquiring a Vocabulary
Writing

DIRECTIONS: Circle the correct word in each sentence.

1. We plan to visit Uncle Harry in one *(week, weak)*.

2. Men's jackets are on *(sail, sale)* today.

3. An accident occurred at the track *(meet, meat)*.

4. Cindy's papers *(blew, blue)* away in the wind.

DIRECTIONS: Write three synonyms for each word.

5. pretty: _____ _____ _____

6. hot: _____ _____ _____

DIRECTIONS: Write three antonyms for each word.

7. pretty: _____ _____ _____

8. hot: _____ _____ _____

DIRECTIONS: Choose the word that means the same or about the same as the underlined word.

9. successful <u>corporation</u>
  - (A) business
  - (B) team
  - (C) person
  - (D) country

10. skilled <u>laborer</u>
  - (F) musician
  - (G) professor
  - (H) worker
  - (J) relative

11. An <u>imaginary</u> story is _____ .
  - (A) biographical
  - (B) fictional
  - (C) actual
  - (D) humorous

12. <u>portable</u> grill
  - (F) movable
  - (G) permanent
  - (H) stationery
  - (J) casual

13. <u>vivid</u> color
  - (A) pale
  - (B) without
  - (C) intense
  - (D) soft

DIRECTIONS: Fill in the circle next to the word that means the opposite of the underlined word.

14. <u>brief</u> description
  - (F) important
  - (G) lengthy
  - (H) short
  - (J) casual

15. <u>employ</u> the workers
  - (A) befriend
  - (B) manage
  - (C) argue with
  - (D) dismiss

16. <u>confident</u> in your abilities

(F) uncertain

(G) assured

(H) proud

(J) neglectful

DIRECTIONS: Read each item. Fill in the circle next to the answer you think is correct.

17. **Unemployment is running high here since the factory closed.**

   In which sentence does the word *running* mean the same thing as in the sentence above?

   (A) Tracy saw the horse running through the field.

   (B) Beth was running the lawn mower.

   (C) Club attendance was running low due to heavy snow.

   (D) Peter is running for class president.

18. **Groaning, he rolled over and planted his feet firmly on the floor.**

   In which sentence does the word *planted* mean the same thing as in the sentence above?

   (F) Jean planted four rows of cucumbers.

   (G) The lawyer claimed that the evidence had been planted.

   (H) The settlers planted new crops.

   (J) Jo planted her feet in the dirt before swinging the bat.

DIRECTIONS: Choose the word that correctly completes both sentences.

19. **Set the package _____ to the side.**
   We had the day _____ .

   (A) over

   (B) off

   (C) apart

   (D) away

20. **Barb put a clean _____ on the bed.**
   Jason washed the cookie _____ after he finished baking.

   (F) pillow

   (G) tray

   (H) sheet

   (J) cover

21. **We _____ nearer to the warmth of the campfire.**
   He _____ the wrong conclusion from the facts that were presented.

   (A) drew

   (B) moved

   (C) identified

   (D) illustrated

22. **They set up a picnic near the _____ of the river.**
   Jenna went to the _____ to deposit the money she earned babysitting.

   (F) coast

   (G) bank

   (H) edge

   (J) store

English Language Arts

| 4.0 |

Using a Variety of Sentence Types

Writing

A **declarative** sentence makes a statement: Ben walked home from school with Jaime.

An **interrogative** sentence asks a question: Will you feed the fish today?

An **exclamatory** sentence shows excitement or emotion: Hey! Stop hitting me!

An **imperative** sentence expresses a command or request: Come to the principal's office now.

DIRECTIONS: Below are eight short paragraphs. For each paragraph, underline the declarative sentences. Then, in each blank, write **IN** if the paragraph also contains an interrogative sentence; write **EX** if it contains an exclamatory sentence; write **IM** if it contains an imperative sentence; write **none** if it contains only declarative sentences.

1. _____ You are on a deserted island: no town, no people—just you and those crazy, noisy seagulls. What are you going to do?

2. _____ Toward the castle she fled. She begged the gatekeeper for entrance. He was as deaf as a gargoyle. He did not hear her cries. Past the stone walls she scurried, the hounds in pursuit.

3. _____ Maggie bit her lip. No use crying about it. She pulled her math homework out of the sink and just stared at her little sister.

4. _____ The music is playing those lovely Christmas tunes, but you're not listening. You can't. You have too many important things to plan. What should you buy for Teddie? Who should you invite to the party? And . . .

5. _____ I'm not proud of it. Really, I am not. But no teacher's ever gotten through to me. I guess I'm just not cut out to be a scholar.

6. _____ Columbus stood on the deck of the ship. Land was on the horizon. Land! Not the edge of the world, not dragons to devour the ship, but the land that would make his fortune . . . his and Spain's.

7. _____ I think Mama forgot me. Otherwise, she would come and find me. Oh, no! I've been bad! Mama said not to go see the toys because I'd get lost. Mama is going to be mad at me!

8. _____ Do not stop reading until you reach the end of this story. What you are about to read is so amazing that you simply *must* hear about it now. So settle back and get ready for the most incredible tale you've ever heard.

DIRECTIONS: On the lines below, write two short paragraphs on topics of your choice. Use all four sentence types at least once in the paragraphs.

9. _____

_____

_____

10. _____

_____

_____

English Language Arts

4.0

Using a Variety of Sentence Structures

Writing

DIRECTIONS: Rewrite each run-on sentence to make it correct. Write **C** if the sentences below are correct as is.

1. Let's ask David to come with us. He knows about a great bike trail.

   _____

   _____

2. I can ride faster than you can let's race to the stop sign.

   _____

   _____

3. I'm thirsty does anyone have some bottled water?

   _____

   _____

4. We need to be careful on the bike trail in-line skaters can appear fast.

   _____

   _____

5. Do you know how to recognize a happy bicyclist? He has bugs in his teeth.

   _____

   _____

6. I love the playground it has great swings.

   _____

   _____

7. When I swing too high, I get sick do you?

   _____

   _____

8. I like the slide the best. I've always liked slides.

   _____

   _____

9. This ride was fun let's do it again tomorrow.

   _____

   _____

DIRECTIONS: Rewrite each sentence fragment below to make it a sentence.

10. found a hidden staircase in the old house

    _____

    _____

11. a mysterious note

    _____

    _____

12. lay behind the creaking door

    _____

    _____

13. the solution to the mystery

    _____

    _____

Name _____   Date _____

5.0

Choosing a Topic
Writing

DIRECTIONS: Read the paragraph that tells about one student's great experience. Then, think about all the good experiences you have ever had to answer each question below.

> My violin competition was one of the best experiences I've ever had. I met people from all over the city. I learned to feel comfortable in front of an audience. I felt good about playing for so many people. When everyone clapped, I felt very proud.

1. Think about all your good experiences. List the top three.

   _____

   _____

   _____

2. For each item you listed in question 1, briefly tell why this experience was so good.

   _____

   _____

   _____

   _____

   _____

   _____

   _____

   _____

   _____

   _____

   _____

3. Pick one of the items you listed in question 1. Outline the three most important things about that experience that you would want to talk about in an essay.

   I. _____

   _____

   _____

   _____

   _____

   II. _____

   _____

   _____

   _____

   III. _____

   _____

   _____

STOP

English Language Arts

5.0

Maintaining a Focus
Writing

DIRECTIONS: Read each paragraph. Fill in the circle next to the sentence that does not belong in the paragraph.

 Clue   Remember, a paragraph should focus on one idea. The correct answer is the one that does not fit the main topic.

1.   (1) In 3000 B.C., the early Egyptian boats were constructed from the *papyrus* plant. (2) With the Egyptians' limited knowledge of navigation, they could only sail with the wind. (3) These reeds, from which early paper was made, could grow to be 20 feet high. (4) The reeds were cut, bundled, and tied together to form the boat.

     (A) Sentence 1
     (B) Sentence 2
     (C) Sentence 3
     (D) Sentence 4

2.   (1) In 1567, Francis Drake, John Hawkins, and other English seamen were on a voyage. (2) They hoped to make a profit by selling smuggled goods to some of the Spanish colonies. (3) On their way back from their voyage, they stopped at a Mexican port. (4) By far, Drake is best known as the first Englishman to sail around the world.

     (F) Sentence 1
     (G) Sentence 2
     (H) Sentence 3
     (J) Sentence 4

3.   (1) In his book, *Over the Top of the World,* Will Steger relates the travels of his research party across the Arctic Ocean from Siberia to Canada in 1994. (2) With a team of 6 people and 33 dogs, Steger set out by dogsled to complete this daring mission. (3) At other times, they boarded their canoes to cross chilly stretches of water. (4) Along the way, the party would exchange dogsleds for canoe sleds because of the breaking ice packs.

     (A) Sentence 1
     (B) Sentence 2
     (C) Sentence 3
     (D) Sentence 4

4.   (1) The "Great Zimbabwe" is one of many stone-walled fortresses built on the Zimbabwean plateau. (2) The Shona spoke a common Bantu language and all were herdsmen and farmers. (3) Researchers believe that the Shona people built this structure over a course of 400 years. (4) More than 18,000 people may have lived in the "Great Zimbabwe."

     (F) Sentence 1
     (G) Sentence 2
     (H) Sentence 3
     (J) Sentence 4

English Language Arts

5.0

Writing Effectively to a Specific Audience
Writing

DIRECTIONS: Read each paragraph. Use the paragraphs to answer the questions.

 Clue Think about the request that is being made in each paragraph. Decide who would most likely be able to help fulfill the request.

My family is planning a trip to Chicago, Illinois. We will arrive on July 1, and we plan to stay for five nights. Can you please help us find a hotel? Also, any information you can share about things to do in Chicago would be appreciated.

1. **Who would be an appropriate person to send this letter to?**
   - (A)   the owner of a restaurant
   - (B)   the mayor of Chicago
   - (C)   a hotel manager
   - (D)   a travel agent

2. **What needed information is missing from this letter?**
   - (F)   the number of nights the family will be staying
   - (G)   the number of hotel rooms needed
   - (H)   where the family is coming from
   - (J)   the type of food the family likes to eat

I would like to make dinner reservations at your restaurant for July 3. We would like to be seated by 7:00. Please let me know if you can accommodate us.

3. **Who would be an appropriate person to send this letter to?**
   - (A)   a relative
   - (B)   a business owner
   - (C)   a restaurant manager
   - (D)   a friend

4. **What needed information is missing from this letter?**
   - (F)   the number of people who want to eat at the restaurant
   - (G)   the type of food the people like to eat
   - (H)   how much money the people plan to spend
   - (J)   the name of the hotel where the people are staying

I'm writing a report in school about the state of Illinois. I think some of the stories about our family moving there would make it more interesting. Can you tell me about the time Grandma lived on the farm?

5. **Who would be an appropriate person to send this letter to?**
   - (A)   a business owner
   - (B)   a state congressman
   - (C)   a travel agent
   - (D)   a relative

 STOP

English Language Arts

6.0

Using Correct
Spelling and Punctuation
Writing

DIRECTIONS: Fill in the circle next to the punctuation mark that is needed in the sentence. Choose "none" if no additional punctuation marks are needed.

1. **The team carried in the bats balls, and gloves.**
   - (A) ;
   - (B) ,
   - (C) :
   - (D) none

2. **"Great catch" yelled the pitcher.**
   - (F) ?
   - (G) .
   - (H) !
   - (J) none

3. **Did you see that foul ball**
   - (A) ?
   - (B) .
   - (C) ,
   - (D) none

4. **Matilda hit a home run.**
   - (F) !
   - (G) "
   - (H) ,
   - (J) none

5. **That's three strikes," said the umpire.**
   - (A) ,
   - (B) "
   - (C) "
   - (D) none

6. **Yes the Fifth Grade Firecrackers won the game.**
   - (F) ,
   - (G) .
   - (H) !
   - (J) none

DIRECTIONS: Fill in the blank with the word that best fits each sentence.

7. **Nikki _____ the class in singing the national anthem.**

   led, lead

8. **Show Brendan _____ we keep the extra towels.**

   where, wear

9. **Jamal, the social studies report is _____ tomorrow!**

   do, dew, due

10. **Call me when _____ my turn to use the computer.**

    it's, its

11. **We can rest when _____ is nothing left to put away.**

    their, there, they're

12. **The keys were _____ on the table this morning.**

    here, hear

13. **Remember, _____ responsible for returning the videos.**

    your, you're

14. **Nathan _____ a chapter of the book every day after dinner.**

    red, read

15. **Aunt Jess _____ the package to me on Monday.**

    sent, cent, scent

STOP

English Language Arts

| 6.0 |

Grammar
Writing

DIRECTIONS: Write the correct form of the verb *lie* or *lay* in each blank.

1. Peter and Zach _____ their towels on the sand.

2. "Zach, where have you _____ our picnic basket?" asked Peter.

3. "I _____ it under the umbrella," replied Zach.

4. Peter decided to _____ on his towel.

DIRECTIONS: Circle the correct word in each sentence.

5. The library is open every day (accept/except) Sunday.

6. How did the speech (affect/effect) the students?

7. Mr. Randolph (accepted/excepted) Mr. Greer's resignation.

8. Everyone (accept/except) my little sister stayed up late.

DIRECTIONS: Choose the best answer.

9. Jeremy taught _____ to play the guitar.
   - (A) hisself
   - (B) itself
   - (C) themselves
   - (D) himself

10. Sheila is _____ than I am.
    - (F) more hungrier
    - (G) hungriest
    - (H) most hungry
    - (J) hungrier

11. The twins can take care of _____ .
    - (A) themselves
    - (B) herself
    - (C) himself
    - (D) yourselves

12. He was the _____ member of the club.
    - (F) more louder
    - (G) louder
    - (H) loudest
    - (J) most loud

13. Lena hurt _____ climbing a tree.
    - (A) itself
    - (B) themselves
    - (C) she
    - (D) herself

14. He is _____ in history than I am.
    - (F) interested
    - (G) interesting
    - (H) most interested
    - (J) more interested

GO

15. Carmina _____ left a chocolate bar on the table.

- (A) angry
- (B) carelessly
- (C) bravely
- (D) have

16. The water _____ in the fountain.

- (F) splash
- (G) having splashed
- (H) splashing
- (J) splashed

17. My mother _____ for three hours.

- (A) drive
- (B) driven
- (C) has drove
- (D) drove

DIRECTIONS: Choose the line that has a usage error. If there is no error, choose "no mistakes."

18.
- (F) George Washington
- (G) are called the father
- (H) of our country.
- (J) no mistakes

19.
- (A) Binoculars are helpful
- (B) because they let you
- (C) observe things closely.
- (D) no mistakes

20.
- (F) We missed the
- (G) baseball game however
- (H) there was a train crossing.
- (J) no mistakes

21.
- (A) The junior high
- (B) play take place on
- (C) Friday and Saturday night.
- (D) no mistakes

22.
- (F) He hasn't never made
- (G) a mistake on any of
- (H) his reading assignments.
- (J) no mistakes

23.
- (A) We haveta get more
- (B) decorations for the hall
- (C) in order to finish.
- (D) no mistakes

24.
- (F) Mrs. Green give
- (G) her fifth-grade class
- (H) a surprise quiz.
- (J) no mistakes

25.
- (A) Carlos and Jeremy are
- (B) best friends who play
- (C) on the same basketball team.
- (D) no mistakes

26.
- (F) Jean and Brenda decided
- (G) to fix the bike themself
- (H) and not ask for help.
- (J) no mistakes

27.
- (A) Did anyone
- (B) find the assignment
- (C) I finish yesterday?
- (D) no mistakes

6.0

Sentence Construction
Writing

DIRECTIONS: Choose the answer that is a complete and correctly written sentence.

1. (A) Scientists spends many hours recording the behavior and habits of animals.

   (B) They search for clues to explain why animals act as they do.

   (C) Through careful observation, the behavior of an animal might could be explained.

   (D) Lemmings, however, does an unexplainable thing.

2. (F) Glass snakes ain't snakes at all.

   (G) They is one of several kinds of lizards that inhabitate the earth.

   (H) Most legless lizards resemble worms, but the glass snake looks very much like a true snake.

   (J) It can break off his tail as easily as a pieces of glass.

DIRECTIONS: Read each answer choice. Fill in the circle for the choice that has an error. If there are no errors, choose "no mistakes."

3. (A) A beach vacation and a ski vacation
   (B) is alike in some ways
   (C) and different in others.
   (D) no mistakes

4. (F) Doing the laundry is a big contribution
   (G) to my family, and I get to put away
   (H) my own clothes exactly the way I like them.
   (J) no mistakes

DIRECTIONS: Read the story. Use it to answer the questions.

(1) Last Saturday, the Wilson family drove to Chicago to watch a Cubs baseball game. (2) The bustling streets around the ballpark were filled with activity. (3) The children spotted a booth outside the stadium that was selling Cubs' baseball caps. (4) They begged their dad to buy each of them a hat. (5) He insisted that they wait until they got inside the park. (6) When they got to the front of the line, the children saw a woman handing out free Cubs' hats. (7) It was free hat day. (8) Mr. Wilson smiled and the children cheered.

5. **How is sentence 1 best written?**

   (A) On a drive to Chicago last Saturday, the Wilson family was watching a Cubs baseball game.

   (B) To watch a Cubs baseball game, the Wilson family drove to Chicago last Saturday.

   (C) Last Saturday, the Wilson family was driving to Chicago and watching a Cubs baseball game.

   (D) as it is

6. **What is the best way to combine sentences 4 and 5 without changing their meaning?**

   (F) They begged their dad to buy each of them a hat, but he insisted that they wait until they got inside the park.

   (G) They begged their dad to buy each of them a hat, because he insisted that they wait until they got inside the park.

   (H) They begged their dad to buy each of them a hat; therefore, he insisted that they wait until they got inside the park.

   (J) Since their dad insisted that they wait until they got inside the park, they begged him to buy each of them a hat.

Name _____ Date _____

English Language Arts

| 4.0–6.0 |

For pages 18–28

Mini-Test 2

Writing

DIRECTIONS: Fill in the circle next to the word that means the same or about the same as the underlined word.

1. Complete the <u>assignment</u>.
- (A) task
- (B) assistant
- (C) design
- (D) office

2. <u>Focus</u> your attention.
- (F) fluctuate
- (G) irritate
- (H) compile
- (J) concentrate

DIRECTIONS: Fill in the circle next to the word that means the opposite of the underlined word.

3. <u>express</u> your thoughts
- (A) yell
- (B) withhold
- (C) summarize
- (D) tell

DIRECTIONS: Choose the best answer.

4. Jason fixed _____ a huge bowl of ice cream.
- (F) him
- (G) himself
- (H) itself
- (J) hisself

5. Which punctuation mark is needed in the following sentence?
Abby asked, Do you want me to serve dinner now?"
- (A) !
- (B) .
- (C) "
- (D) none

DIRECTIONS: Choose the answer that is a complete and correctly written sentence.

6.
- (F) The fire company responded quick to the call for help.
- (G) My family usually contributes to the fund drive for the fire company.
- (H) They were happily to see the ambulance.
- (J) Nicely people on the ambulance squad.

7.
- (A) Art class once a week with students in another class.
- (B) Entering a painting in the show.
- (C) Drawing and painting enjoyed by many young people.
- (D) The pot you made is beautiful.

DIRECTIONS: Write a paragraph about your favorite dessert. Use at least one interrogative and one exclamatory sentence.

8. _____
_____
_____
_____
_____
_____

STOP

Name _____ Date _____

English Language Arts
7.0

Using Print and Nonprint Sources
Research

DIRECTIONS: Use the library or Internet to find two sources on a topic of your choice. One of the sources should be print (book, magazine article, etc.). The second should be nonprint (film or videotape, photo collection, audio recording). Examine the sources. Then, complete the page below.

 Clue

If you are having trouble finding a topic, try researching baseball in the 1920s, the life of an American pioneer, the 1903 San Francisco earthquake, or current teenage fashions in the United States.

Print Source

Description of print source:

_____

_____

_____

Main idea:

_____

_____

Details that support main idea:

_____

_____

_____

_____

Nonprint Source

Description of nonprint source:

_____

_____

_____

Main idea:

_____

_____

Details that support main idea:

_____

_____

_____

_____

Briefly describe some things you learned from the print source that you did not learn from the nonprint source. Then, describe some things you learned from the nonprint source that you did not learn from the print source.

_____

_____

_____

 STOP

English Language Arts

8.0

Using Reference Materials
Research

DIRECTIONS: Use the sample thesaurus entry below to answer the questions.

> **supine,** *adj.* **1.** flat, flat on one's back, horizontal, lounge, recline.
> **2.** inactive, motionless, lazy, lifeless.
> **supple,** *adj.* **1.** flexible, bendable, pliant; elastic, stretchable.
> **2.** limber, loose-limbed, double-jointed.
> **3.** yielding, unresistant, passive.
> **4.** changeable, movable, agreeable, willing.

1. The words listed in this thesaurus entry are both _____ .

   Ⓐ nouns
   Ⓑ verbs
   Ⓒ adjectives
   Ⓓ adverbs

2. Write three synonyms for the word *supple.*

   _____

   _____

3. Write one antonym for the word *supple.*

   _____

4. Even if you didn't know the meaning of *supine* before looking in the thesaurus, how would you define it after reading this entry? Write a definition.

   _____

   _____

   _____

DIRECTIONS: A **bibliography** is a list of the books and articles a writer uses for reference when writing a report. A bibliography tells interested readers where to find more information on the report's topic. The bibliography below was prepared by someone who wrote a report called *The Wild West.* Read the bibliography and use it to answer questions 5–9.

> **Book**
> Alter, Judy. Author
> *Growing Up in the Old West*
> Watts, 1999
>
> **Encyclopedia Article**
> "Pioneers in the Wild West"
> *McMahon Encyclopedia*, 2002 edition
> vol. 12, pp. 278–282.
>
> **Magazine Article**
> Tripp, John R. Author
> "Exploring the American West."
> *The U.S. Experience*
> vol. 114 (April 1998): 25–32.

5. What three types of references did the writer use to write his or her report?

   _____

   _____

   _____

6. Which of these references was published most recently?

   _____

7. In what volume of the encyclopedia did the writer find his or her information about pioneers in the Wild West?

   _____

8. On what pages did the magazine article appear?

_____

9. If you wanted to find out what it was like to be a child in the Old West, what would be the best reference?

_____

DIRECTIONS: Use the sample dictionary entries and the Pronunciation Guide to answer questions 10–15.

> **camp** /'kamp/ *n.* **1.** a place, usually away from cities, where tents or simple buildings are put up to provide shelter for people working or vacationing there **2.** a place, usually in the country, for recreation or instruction during the summer months [goes to summer camp each July] **3.** a group of people who work to promote a certain idea or thought or who work together in support of another person *v.* **4.** to live temporarily in a camp or outdoors.
> **cam·paign** /kăm-'pān/ *n.* **1.** a series of military operations that make up a distinct period during a war **2.** a series of activities designed to bring about a desired outcome [an election campaign] *v.* **3.** to conduct a campaign
> **cam·pus** /'kam-pᵊs/ *n.* **1.** the grounds and buildings of a school
>
> Pronunciation Guide:
> **a**sh, st**ā**y, ə = a in *alone* and u in *circus*, w**e**t, **ē**asy, h**i**t, h**ī**de, f**o**x, g**ō**, b**u**t, m**ū**sic

10. The "u" in *campus* sounds most like the vowel sound in _____ .

- (F) but
- (G) music
- (H) circus
- (J) wet

11. Which definition best fits the word *camp* as it is used in the sentence below?

The field workers lived in a *camp* a mile away from the farm.

- (A) 1
- (B) 2
- (C) 3
- (D) 4

12. How many syllables are in the word *campaign?*

- (F) 1
- (G) 2
- (H) 3
- (J) 4

13. In which of these sentences is *camp* used as a verb?

- (A) The governor's camp worked through the night to prepare her acceptance speech.
- (B) Della will go to music camp in July.
- (C) The hike back to camp took three hours.
- (D) The family will camp in Yosemite this spring.

14. What part of speech is the word *campus?*

- (F) verb
- (G) noun
- (H) adjective
- (J) adverb

15. Look at the words in the sample dictionary. Which guide words would appear on the dictionary page on which these words are located?

- (A) campground–candle
- (B) camera–campfire
- (C) camisole–canal
- (D) camper–campsite

Name _____ Date _____

Mini-Test 3

Research

DIRECTIONS: Use the dictionary entries to answer questions 1–2.

save [sāv] *v.* **1.** to rescue from harm or danger **2.** to keep in a safe condition **3.** to set aside for future use; store **4.** to avoid
saving [sā'-vǐng] *v.* **1.** rescuing from harm or danger **2.** avoiding excess spending; economy. *n.* **1.** something saved

1. **The "a" in the word *saving* sounds most like the "a" in the word _____ .**
   - (A) pat
   - (B) ape
   - (C) heated
   - (D) naughty

2. **Which sentence uses *save* in the same way as definition number 3?**
   - (F) Firefighters save lives.
   - (G) She saves half of all she earns.
   - (H) Going by jet saves eight hours of driving.
   - (J) The life jacket saved the boy from drowning.

DIRECTIONS: Choose the best answer.

3. **Where would you find information about the sources an author used to write a book?**
   - (A) title page
   - (B) index
   - (C) bibliography
   - (D) table of contents

DIRECTIONS: Use the sample thesaurus to answer questions 4–6. Choose the best synonym to replace the underlined word in each sentence.

> **head** [hed] *n.* **1.** skull, scalp, *noggin **2.** leader, commander, director, chief, manager **3.** top, summit, peak **4.** front **5.** toilet, restroom (on a boat)
> **head** [hed] *v.* **1.** lead, command, direct, supervise
>
> **Key:** *n.* noun, *v.* verb, *slang

4. **The brain is inside the <u>head</u>.**
   - (F) front
   - (G) top
   - (H) summit
   - (J) skull

5. **Captain Blaine was the <u>head</u> of the army.**
   - (A) commander
   - (B) top
   - (C) peak
   - (D) front

6. **How is the underlined word used in this sentence?**

   She was chosen to <u>head</u> the Art Club.
   - (F) noun
   - (G) adverb
   - (H) slang
   - (J) verb

9.0

Comparing Texts From Different Cultures
Cultural and Social Language Use

DIRECTIONS: Read the passage and answer the questions that follow.

Walks All Over the Sky
Back when the sky was completely dark, there was a chief with two sons, a younger son, *One Who Walks All Over the Sky,* and an older son, *Walking About Early.* The younger son was sad to see the sky always so dark, so he made a mask out of wood and pitch (the sun) and lit it on fire. Each day, he travels across the sky. At night, he sleeps below the horizon and when he snores sparks fly from the mask and make the stars. The older brother became jealous. To impress their father, he smeared fat and charcoal on his face (the moon) and makes his own path across the sky.
—From the *Tsimshian of the Pacific Northwest*

The Porcupine
Once Porcupine and Beaver argued about the seasons. Porcupine wanted five winter months. He held up one hand and showed his five fingers. He said, "Let the winter months be the same in number as the fingers on my hand." Beaver said, "No," and held up his tail, which had many cracks or scratches on it. He said, "Let the winter months be the same in number as the scratches on my tail." They argued more, and Porcupine got angry and bit off his thumb. Then, holding up his hand with the four fingers, he said, "There must be only four winter months." Beaver was afraid and gave in. For this reason, today porcupines have four claws on each foot.
—From the *Tahltan: Teit, Journal of American Folk-Lore,* xxxii, 226

Both of these stories are from different cultures. However, they both try to explain something.

1. **What is explained in the first story?**

   _____

   _____

2. **What is explained in the second story?**

   _____

   _____

3. **Who are the two characters in the first story? In the second story?**

   _____

   _____

4. **How is the relationship between the characters in the first story and the characters in the second story alike?**

   _____

   _____

   _____

Name _____ Date _____

English Language Arts

Writing About Community
Cultural and Social Language Use

DIRECTIONS: Write three short paragraphs about what things you think need to be improved in your community. Structure your composition as follows.

Paragraph 1: Choose at least three things that you think could use improvement. Describe them.
Paragraph 2: Give reasons why you think these things should be improved.
Paragraph 3: Conclude by explaining what you personally would do to make these improvements.

_____

_____

_____

_____

_____

_____

_____

_____

_____

_____

_____

_____

_____

_____

_____

_____

_____

_____

_____

_____

_____

English Language Arts

12.0 # Writing to Communicate
Cultural and Social Language Use

DIRECTIONS: Read the paragraph below about how to plant a seed. Then, think of something you know how to do well. Write a paragraph to your classmates that explains how to do it. Keep your audience in mind as you write your paragraph. Use transition words such as *first, next, then, finally,* and *last.* Use details to explain how you learned to do this activity and why you enjoy it.

Example:

>   I found out how to plant a seed and make it grow. First, I found a spot where the plant would get the right amount of sunlight. Next, I dug a hole, put the seed into the soil, and then covered the seed with soil. Then, I watered the seed. After a couple weeks, it began to grow into a beautiful plant.

_____

_____

_____

_____

_____

_____

_____

_____

_____

_____

_____

_____

_____

_____

_____

_____

_____

English Language Arts

9.0–12.0

For pages 34–36

Mini-Test 4

Cultural and Social Language Use

DIRECTIONS: Write a paragraph about your favorite way to spend a day. Give details about why these activities are your favorites. Use words that express your feelings.

_____

_____

_____

_____

_____

_____

_____

_____

_____

_____

_____

_____

_____

_____

_____

_____

_____

_____

_____

_____

_____

_____

_____

_____

_____

STOP

How Am I Doing?

Mini-Test 1 Page 17 **Number Correct**	8 answers correct	**Great Job!** Move on to the section test on page 40.
	5–7 answers correct	**You're almost there!** But you still need a little practice. Review practice pages 9–16 before moving on to the section test on page 40.
	0–4 answers correct	**Oops!** Time to review what you have learned and try again. Review the practice section on pages 9–16. Then, retake the test on page 17. Now, move on to the section test on page 40.
Mini-Test 2 Page 29 **Number Correct**	8 answers correct	**Awesome!** Move on to the section test on page 40.
	5–7 answers correct	**You're almost there!** But you still need a little practice. Review practice pages 18–28 before moving on to the section test on page 40.
	0–4 answers correct	**Oops!** Time to review what you have learned and try again. Review the practice section on pages 18–28. Then, retake the test on page 29. Now, move on to the section test on page 40.
Mini-Test 3 Page 33 **Number Correct**	6 answers correct	**Great Job!** Move on to the section test on page 40.
	5 answers correct	**You're almost there!** But you still need a little practice. Review practice pages 30–32 before moving on to the section test on page 40.
	0–4 answers correct	**Oops!** Time to review what you have learned and try again. Review the practice section on pages 30–32. Then, retake the test on page 33. Now, move on to the section test on page 40.

How Am I Doing?

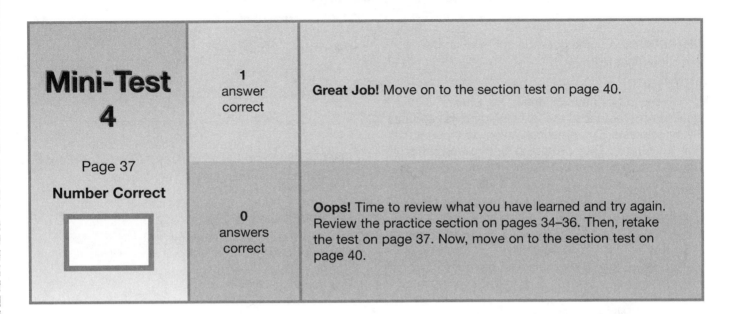

Mini-Test 4 Page 37 **Number Correct**	1 answer correct	**Great Job!** Move on to the section test on page 40.
	0 answers correct	**Oops!** Time to review what you have learned and try again. Review the practice section on pages 34–36. Then, retake the test on page 37. Now, move on to the section test on page 40.

Final English Language Arts Test
for pages 9–37

DIRECTIONS: Read the passage and answer the questions that follow.

To pay off its national debts, the British government increased the taxes paid on its products by its colonists. The American colonists thought this was very unfair. They protested by throwing British tea and merchandise into Boston Harbor.

1. **Which of the following best describes the passage?**

   Ⓐ It is made up or fantasized.

   Ⓑ It contains opinions, but not facts.

   Ⓒ Its main purpose is to entertain.

   Ⓓ Its main purpose is to inform.

2. **This passage belongs to which genre?**

   Ⓕ fable

   Ⓖ poetry

   Ⓗ biography

   Ⓙ nonfiction

DIRECTIONS: Read the paragraph. Choose the word that best fits in each numbered blank.

The armadillo is _____**(3)**_____ in several ways. First, the female gives birth to four babies, and they are always the same sex. Second, when an armadillo is cornered and cannot escape to its _____**(4)**_____ or quickly dig itself into the ground, it rolls itself into a tight, protective ball. This is possible because of the joined overlapping plates of its shell. The armadillo also tucks in its head and feet.

3. Ⓐ honored

   Ⓑ unusual

   Ⓒ motivated

   Ⓓ typical

4. Ⓕ burrow

   Ⓖ vehicle

   Ⓗ porch

   Ⓙ dormitory

DIRECTIONS: Read the sentences. Choose the word that correctly completes both sentences

5. **The dog caught the _____ .**

   Our school has a formal _____ .

   Ⓐ ball

   Ⓑ dance

   Ⓒ stick

   Ⓓ event

DIRECTIONS: Choose the word that means the same or about the same as the underlined word.

6. **a bundle of goods**

   Ⓕ sweater

   Ⓖ burden

   Ⓗ rumble

   Ⓙ package

7. **restore the wood**

   Ⓐ repair

   Ⓑ retread

   Ⓒ relieve

   Ⓓ reduce

GO

Name _____   Date _____

DIRECTIONS: Choose the word that means the opposite of the underlined word.

8. <u>contemporary</u> art

    (F) modern

    (G) ancient

    (H) imaginative

    (J) folksy

9. <u>scamper</u> away

    (A) waltz

    (B) crawl

    (C) run

    (D) sprint

DIRECTIONS: Choose the answer that is a complete and correctly written sentence.

10.   (F) He didn't hurt hisself when he bumped his head.

    (G) Theys have some concerns about the homework.

    (H) Me and her practiced writing our name backward.

    (J) Rika and I went in-line skating for three hours yesterday.

DIRECTIONS: Read the paragraph below. Find the sentence that does not belong in the paragraph.

    (1) Gregory's father worked for the Wildlife Department. **(2)** One day, he came to Gregory's class carrying a small cage. **(3)** When Gregory's father left, the students discussed his visit. **(4)** When he opened the top of the cage, a furry little raccoon popped out.

11.   (A) Sentence 1

    (B) Sentence 2

    (C) Sentence 3

    (D) Sentence 4

DIRECTIONS: Decide which punctuation mark, if any, is needed in the underlined part of the sentence.

12. "This is <u>fun,</u> answered Lettie.

    (F) ,

    (G) ?

    (H) "

    (J) none

DIRECTIONS: Choose the word or phrase that best completes the sentence.

13. I saw the _____ tree in the world in California.

    (A) tallest

    (B) most tallest

    (C) most taller

    (D) tall

DIRECTIONS: Choose the line that has a usage error. If there is no error, choose "no mistake."

14.   (F) The library have a room for music.

    (G) In the room, you can listen to tapes.

    (H) The room has lots of books about music.

    (J) no mistake

15.   (A) Chang has picked up her heavy backpack.

    (B) She carry that backpack everywhere.

    (C) It has all her art supplies in it.

    (D) no mistake

DIRECTIONS: Use the dictionary entry below to answer questions 16–17.

beam [bēm] *n.* **1.** a squared-off log used to support a building **2.** a ray of light **3.** the wooden roller in a loom *v.* **1.** to shine **2.** to smile broadly

16. **Which sentence uses the word *beam* in the same way as the first definition of the noun?**
  - (F) The beam held up the plaster ceiling.
  - (G) The beam of sunlight warmed the room.
  - (H) She moved the beam before she added a row of wool.
  - (J) The bright stars beam in the night sky.

17. **The "ea" in the word *beam* sounds most like the "ea" in the word _____ .**
  - (A) beautiful
  - (B) great
  - (C) treat
  - (D) tear

18. **If you wanted to find a synonym for the word *attractive,* which reference would you use?**
  - (F) a dictionary
  - (G) an encyclopedia
  - (H) an atlas
  - (J) a thesaurus

DIRECTIONS: Read the passage and answer the questions that follow.

The Story of Arachne

Long ago in a far away country lived a young woman named Arachne. She was not rich or beautiful, but she had one great talent. Arachne could weave the most beautiful cloth anyone had ever seen. Everyone in Arachne's village talked about her wonderful cloth, and soon she became famous. But as her fame grew, so did her pride.

"No one else can weave as well as I can," Arachne boasted. "Not even the goddess Minerva could make anything so lovely and fine."

Now, Minerva wove cloth for all the gods. She was proud of her weaving too and thought that no human being could ever match her skills. Soon, Arachne's words reached Minerva's ears, and the goddess became angry.

"So, the human woman thinks she is better than I!" Minerva roared. "We will see about that!"

Minerva searched the countryside until she came upon Arachne's home. Minerva called to Arachne and challenged her to a contest. "Let us both weave a length of cloth. We will see whose is the most beautiful."

Arachne agreed. She set up two looms, and she and Minerva went to work. The goddess wove cloth of all the colors of the rainbow. It sparkled in the sun and floated on the breeze like a butterfly. But Arachne wove cloth that sparkled like gold and jewels. The villagers were dazzled by Arachne's cloth. When Minerva inspected it, she knew Arachne was the best weaver.

Minerva was enraged. She took out a jar of magic water and sprinkled it on Arachne. Instantly, poor Arachne began to change. She shrank smaller and smaller until she could almost not be seen. She grew more arms and became covered in fine brown hair. When it was all over, Arachne had become a tiny brown spider. Arachne would never boast again, but she would spend the rest of her life weaving fine webs.

19. **This passage explains _____ .**
  - (A) how to weave cloth
  - (B) why spiders weave webs
  - (C) how to turn a person into a spider
  - (D) why it is wrong to be boastful

20. **Which genre is this passage?**
  - (F) biography
  - (G) myth
  - (H) nonfiction
  - (J) poetry

Final English Language Arts Test

Answer Sheet

1 Ⓐ Ⓑ Ⓒ Ⓓ
2 Ⓕ Ⓖ Ⓗ Ⓙ
3 Ⓐ Ⓑ Ⓒ Ⓓ
4 Ⓕ Ⓖ Ⓗ Ⓙ
5 Ⓐ Ⓑ Ⓒ Ⓓ
6 Ⓕ Ⓖ Ⓗ Ⓙ
7 Ⓐ Ⓑ Ⓒ Ⓓ
8 Ⓕ Ⓖ Ⓗ Ⓙ
9 Ⓐ Ⓑ Ⓒ Ⓓ
10 Ⓕ Ⓖ Ⓗ Ⓙ

11 Ⓐ Ⓑ Ⓒ Ⓓ
12 Ⓕ Ⓖ Ⓗ Ⓙ
13 Ⓐ Ⓑ Ⓒ Ⓓ
14 Ⓕ Ⓖ Ⓗ Ⓙ
15 Ⓐ Ⓑ Ⓒ Ⓓ
16 Ⓕ Ⓖ Ⓗ Ⓙ
17 Ⓐ Ⓑ Ⓒ Ⓓ
18 Ⓕ Ⓖ Ⓗ Ⓙ
19 Ⓐ Ⓑ Ⓒ Ⓓ
20 Ⓕ Ⓖ Ⓗ Ⓙ

Mathematics Standards

Standard 1—Number and Operations *(See pages 45–49.)*
- A. Understand numbers, ways of representing numbers, relationships among numbers, and number systems.
- B. Understand meanings of operations and how they relate to one another.
- C. Compute fluently and make reasonable estimates.

Standard 2—Algebra *(See pages 50–53.)*
- A. Understand patterns, relations, and functions.
- B. Represent and analyze mathematical situations and structures using algebraic symbols.
- C. Use mathematical models to represent and understand quantitative relationships.
- D. Analyze change in various contexts.

Standard 3—Geometry *(See pages 55–60.)*
- A. Analyze characteristics and properties of two- and three-dimensional shapes and develop mathematical arguments about geometric relationships.
- B. Specify locations and describe spatial relationships using coordinate geometry and other representational systems.
- C. Apply transformations and use symmetry to analyze mathematical situations.
- D. Use visualization, spatial reasoning, and geometric modeling to solve problems.

Standard 4—Measurement *(See pages 61–64.)*
- A. Understand measurable attributes of objects and the units, systems, and processes of measurement.
- B. Apply appropriate techniques, tools, and formulas to determine measurement.

Standard 5—Data Analysis and Probability *(See pages 66–69.)*
- A. Formulate questions that can be addressed with data and collect, organize, and display relevant data to answer them.
- B. Select and use appropriate statistical methods to analyze data.
- C. Develop and evaluate inferences and predictions that are based on data.
- D. Understand and apply basic concepts of probability.

Standard 6—Process *(See pages 70–73.)*
- A. Problem Solving
- B. Reasoning and Proof
- C. Communication
- D. Connections
- E. Representation

Name _____ Date _____

Mathematics

1.A

Comparing and Ordering Fractions

Number and Operations

DIRECTIONS: Write $<$, $>$, or $=$ in the provided box to make the statement true.

1. $\frac{1}{2}$ ☐ $\frac{1}{4}$

2. $\frac{1}{12}$ ☐ $\frac{1}{2}$

3. $\frac{1}{7}$ ☐ $\frac{1}{8}$

4. $\frac{2}{8}$ ☐ $\frac{1}{4}$

5. $\frac{1}{10}$ ☐ $\frac{1}{11}$

6. $\frac{3}{4}$ ☐ $\frac{9}{12}$

7. $\frac{1}{6}$ ☐ $\frac{1}{12}$

8. $\frac{3}{6}$ ☐ $\frac{1}{2}$

9. $\frac{1}{4}$ ☐ $\frac{1}{6}$

10. $\frac{1}{3}$ ☐ $\frac{1}{5}$

11. $\frac{1}{3}$ ☐ $\frac{3}{9}$

12. $\frac{1}{9}$ ☐ $\frac{1}{4}$

DIRECTIONS: Choose the best answer.

13. Place these fractions in order from smallest to largest:

    1/5, 1/12, 1/4, 1/8, 1/2.

    Ⓐ 1/12, 1/2, 1/4, 1/5, 1/8

    Ⓑ 1/2, 1/12, 1/4, 1/5, 1/8

    Ⓒ 1/2, 1/4, 1/5, 1/8, 1/12

    Ⓓ 1/12, 1/8, 1/5, 1/4, 1/2

14. Place these fractions in order from largest to smallest:

    1/11, 1/3, 1/9, 1/7, 1/6.

    Ⓕ 1/11, 1/9, 1/7, 1/6, 1/3

    Ⓖ 1/3, 1/6, 1/7, 1/9, 1/11

    Ⓗ 1/11, 1/9, 1/6, 1/7, 1/3

    Ⓙ 1/3, 1/7, 1/6, 1/9, 1/11

15. Place these fractions in order from smallest to largest:

    1/6, 1/26, 1/16, 1/36, 1/64.

    Ⓐ 1/64, 1/36, 1/26, 1/16, 1/6

    Ⓑ 1/16, 1/26, 1/36, 1/64, 1/6

    Ⓒ 1/6, 1/16, 1/26, 1/36, 1/64

    Ⓓ 1/64, 1/6, 1/16, 1/26, 1/36

16. Place these fractions in order from largest to smallest:

    1/24, 1/32, 1/16, 1/12, 1/4.

    Ⓕ 1/12, 1/16, 1/24, 1/32, 1/4

    Ⓖ 1/32, 1/24, 1/16, 1/12, 1/4

    Ⓗ 1/4, 1/32, 1/24, 1/16, 1/12

    Ⓙ 1/4, 1/12, 1/16, 1/24, 1/32

1.A

Describing Integers in Familiar Applications
Number and Operations

DIRECTIONS: Choose the best answer.

1. Saturday   Sunday

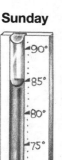

How did the temperature change between Saturday and Sunday? On Sunday it was

- (A) 5 degrees cooler than Saturday.
- (B) 10 degrees cooler than Saturday.
- (C) 5 degrees warmer than Saturday.
- (D) 10 degrees warmer than Saturday.

2. What temperature does this thermometer show?

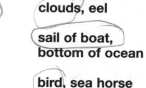

- (F) 87° F
- (G) 82° F
- (H) 80° F
- (J) 78° F

DIRECTIONS: For questions 3–5, use the chart in the right column.

3. Write an integer to represent approximately where the following are located:

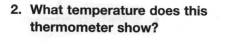

-2 porpoise   -7 sea horse

4 bird   -4 octopus

-9 eel   6 clouds

3 flag on sailboat   -6 jellyfish

4. In each pair, circle the item that represents the greater integer.

(sea horse, porpoise)   (clouds, eel)

(eel, flag)   (sail of boat,) bottom of ocean

(buoy, octopus)   (bird, sea horse)

5. Put the following items in order from least to greatest by the integers they represent:

jellyfish, buoy, eel, porpoise, bird, octopus, clouds

eel, jellyfish, octopus, porpoise, bouy, bird, clouds.

Name _____   Date _____

Mathematics

| 1.A |

Equivalent Numbers
Number and Operations

DIRECTIONS: Choose the best answer.

Example:

If 87% of the students passed the test, how many passed if there were 100 students?

(A) 13

(B) 87

(C) 100

(D) 43

Answer: (B)

1. 30 people at the concert left early. There were a total of 100 people there at the beginning of the concert. Which decimal shows how many left early?

(A) 1.00

(B) 0.70

(C) 0.30

(D) 0.00

2. 3,206 is equivalent to

(F) 3,000 + 200 + 6

(G) 3,000 + 20 + 6

(H) 320 + 6

(J) 32 + 06

3. Which of the following is not equivalent to $\frac{1}{2}$?

(A) 50%

(B) 0.5

(C) 25%

(D) $\frac{5}{10}$

4. Which of the following is not equivalent to $\frac{3}{4}$?

(F) $\frac{9}{12}$

(G) 75%

(H) 0.75

(J) 0.34

5. Which of the following fractions is equivalent to 25%?

(A) $\frac{1}{8}$

(B) $\frac{1}{4}$

(C) $\frac{1}{2}$

(D) $\frac{3}{4}$

6. $\frac{9}{4}$ can also be written as

(F) $9\frac{1}{4}$

(G) $4\frac{1}{9}$

(H) $2\frac{1}{4}$

(J) $\frac{4}{9}$

STOP

Mathematics

1.B

Distributive Property
Number and Operations

DIRECTIONS: Use the distributive property to rewrite the following expressions. Then, use the correct order of operations to solve both sides and check your answers.

Example:

The **distributive property** is used when there is a combination of multiplication over addition or subtraction.

$5(3 + 6) = 5 \times 3 + 5 \times 6$ $16 - 6 = (8 \times 2) - (3 \times 2)$
$5 \times 9 = 15 + 30$ $10 = (8 - 3)2$
$45 = 45$ $10 = 10$

1. $2(6 + 3) =$

2. $12 + 9 =$

3. $4(9 - 1) =$

4. $18 - 6 =$

5. $(15 - 3)2 =$

6. $(7 + 5)8 =$

7. $25 - 15 =$

8. $3(5 + 6) =$

9. $8 + 12 =$

Mathematics

| 1.C |

Multiplying and Dividing
Number and Operations

DIRECTIONS: Choose the best answer.

Clue You can check your answers in a division problem by multiplying your answer by the divisor.

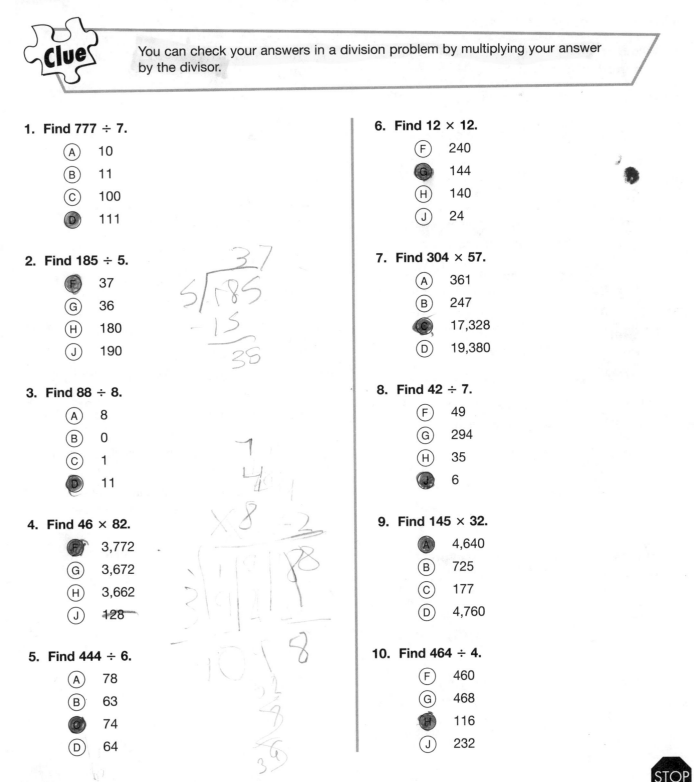

1. **Find 777 ÷ 7.**
   - (A) 10
   - (B) 11
   - (C) 100
   - (D) 111

2. **Find 185 ÷ 5.**
   - (F) 37
   - (G) 36
   - (H) 180
   - (J) 190

3. **Find 88 ÷ 8.**
   - (A) 8
   - (B) 0
   - (C) 1
   - (D) 11

4. **Find 46 × 82.**
   - (F) 3,772
   - (G) 3,672
   - (H) 3,662
   - (J) 128

5. **Find 444 ÷ 6.**
   - (A) 78
   - (B) 63
   - (C) 74
   - (D) 64

6. **Find 12 × 12.**
   - (F) 240
   - (G) 144
   - (H) 140
   - (J) 24

7. **Find 304 × 57.**
   - (A) 361
   - (B) 247
   - (C) 17,328
   - (D) 19,380

8. **Find 42 ÷ 7.**
   - (F) 49
   - (G) 294
   - (H) 35
   - (J) 6

9. **Find 145 × 32.**
   - (A) 4,640
   - (B) 725
   - (C) 177
   - (D) 4,760

10. **Find 464 ÷ 4.**
    - (F) 460
    - (G) 468
    - (H) 116
    - (J) 232

STOP

Name _____   Date _____

Representing and Analyzing Patterns
Algebra

DIRECTIONS: Choose the best answer.

1. **Which of the following rules would give this pattern: 1, 2, 3, 5, 8, 13?**
   - (A) Add the previous two numbers to get the next number.
   - (B) Subtract by decreasing consecutive integers.
   - ● Add by increasing consecutive integers.
   - (D) Add 2 and subtract 1.

	C1	C2	C3	C4	C5
R1	20	40	60	80	100
R2	18	36	54	72	90
R3	15	30	45	60	75
R4	11	22	33	44	55
R5	6	12	18	24	30

2. **Which column has the rule of: Subtract by increasing consecutive integers?**
   - (F) C1
   - (G) C2
   - (H) C3
   - (J) C4

3. **Which column has the rule of: Subtract by integers increasing by threes?**
   - (A) C1
   - (B) C2
   - (C) C3
   - (D) C4

4. **Which column has the rule of: Subtract by integers increasing by fives?**
   - (F) C1
   - (G) C2
   - (H) C3
   - (J) C5

5. **Which column has the rule of: Subtract by integers increasing by twos?**
   - (A) C1
   - (B) C2
   - (C) C3
   - (D) C4

6. **What is the rule for the rows?**
   - (F) The numbers increase across by a factor of two.
   - (G) The numbers increase across by the first number in the row.
   - (H) The numbers increase across by a factor of three.
   - (J) The numbers increase across by the sum of the first two numbers.

Mathematics

2.B

Working With Variables
Algebra

DIRECTIONS: Choose the best answer.

Example:

A factory has 314 workers. The owner gave a total bonus of $612,300. Which number sentence shows how to find the amount of bonus money each worker received? Let b = amount of bonus money.

(A) $b + 314 = \$612,300$

(B) $b \times 314 = \$612,300$

(C) $b - 314 = \$612,300$

(D) $b \div 314 = \$612,300$

Answer: (B)

 Clue   Read each question carefully. Look for key words and numbers that will help you find the answers.

1. What number does a equal to make all the number sentences shown true?

   $6 \times a = 12$; $a \times 10 = 20$; $9 \times a = 18$

   (A) 3

   (B) 4

   (C) 2

   (D) 5

2. Which statement is true about the value of z in the equation: $6,896 \div 1,000 = z$?

   (F) z is less than 5.

   (G) z is between 5 and 6.

   (H) z is equal to 6.

   (J) z is between 6 and 7.

3. What is the value of m in the equation: $81 \div 9 = (9 \div 3) \times (9 \div m)$?

   (A) 81

   (B) 27

   (C) 9

   (D) 3

4. Which of the following equations does not belong to the same family or group as the equation: $c \times 9 = 36$?

   (F) $36 \div c = 9$

   (G) $36 \div c = 6$

   (H) $36 \div 9 = c$

   (J) $9 \times c = 36$

5. Suppose you wanted to double a number n and then add 10 to it. Which expression would you use?

   (A) $(n \times 2) + 10$

   (B) $n + 2 + 10$

   (C) $n \times 2 \times 10$

   (D) $(2 \times 10) + n$

6. What value of r makes these number sentences true?

   $r + 21 = 30$; $63 \div 7 = r$

   (F) 19

   (G) 8

   (H) 11

   (J) 9

STOP

2.C

Using Charts and Graphs
Algebra

DIRECTIONS: Choose the best answer.

There are five classes in the fifth grade at the Tropicana School: Classes 5-1, 5-2, 5-3, 5-4, and 5-5. A different teacher teaches each class. The number of students in each class is represented by the pictograph below. Each ☺ means 8 students. Use the following chart for all of the questions.

Class	Teacher	Number of Students
5-1	Miss Apple	☺ ☺ ☺ ◖
5-2	Mr. Kiwi	☺ ☺ ☺ ◔
5-3	Ms. Melon	☺ ☺ ☺ ◿
5-4	Mr. Cranberry	☺ ☺ ◖
5-5	Miss Mango	☺ ☺ ☺ ☺

1. How many students does ☺ ☺ represent?
   - Ⓐ 16
   - Ⓑ 8
   - Ⓒ 4
   - Ⓓ 2

2. How many students does ☺ ◖ represent?
   - Ⓕ 16
   - Ⓖ 8
   - Ⓗ 12
   - Ⓙ 2

3. How many students does ☺ ◿ represent?
   - Ⓐ 2
   - Ⓑ 10
   - Ⓒ 6
   - Ⓓ 8

4. How many students are in Mr. Cranberry's class and Miss Mango's class combined?
   - Ⓕ 7
   - Ⓖ 13
   - Ⓗ 52
   - Ⓙ 25

5. Which teacher has 30 students?
   - Ⓐ Miss Apple
   - Ⓑ Mr. Kiwi
   - Ⓒ Ms. Melon
   - Ⓓ Mr. Cranberry

6. How many more students are in Miss Apple's class than in Ms. Melon's class?
   - Ⓕ 1
   - Ⓖ 2
   - Ⓗ 3
   - Ⓙ 4

7. Mr. Kiwi divides his students into 5 equal teams. How many students are in each team?
   - Ⓐ 8
   - Ⓑ 5
   - Ⓒ 6
   - Ⓓ 4

Mathematics

2.D

Rates of Change
Algebra

DIRECTIONS: Use the patterns below to answer the questions.

1. **Look for a pattern in the following shapes. Fill in the table.**

Pattern A:

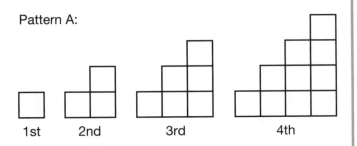

1st   2nd   3rd   4th

Shape	Number of Tiles
1st	1
2nd	3
3rd	6
4th	10
5th	
6th	
7th	
8th	

2. **Explain how the pattern grows.**

_____

_____

_____

_____

3. **If the pattern continues, how many tiles will be in the 10th shape?** _____

4. **Doug is planning a party. He has to plan where to seat people. He can seat one guest on each open end of a table. He must group the tables in rectangles. Look for a pattern and fill in the table below.**

Pattern B:

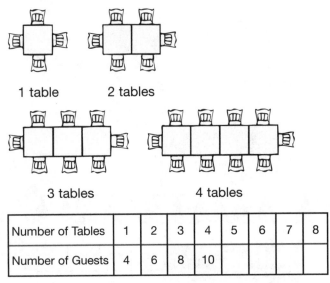

1 table   2 tables

3 tables   4 tables

Number of Tables	1	2	3	4	5	6	7	8
Number of Guests	4	6	8	10				

5. **Explain how the pattern grows.**

_____

_____

_____

_____

_____

6. **If the pattern continues, how many guests will be able to sit at 10 tables?** _____

Mathematics

1.0–2.0

For pages 45–53

Mini-Test 1

Number and Operations; Algebra

DIRECTIONS: Choose the best answer.

1. Which of the following is equivalent to $\frac{3}{10}$?

   (A) $\frac{1}{3}$

   (B) $\frac{2}{9}$

   (C) $\frac{6}{20}$

   (D) $\frac{7}{30}$

2. $780 \div 12 =$

   (F) 65

   (G) 82

   (H) 73

   (J) 91

Shape	1st	2nd	3rd	4th
Number of triangles	2	4	6	

3. What is the pattern for the number of triangles above?

   (A) The number of triangles increases by three each time.

   (B) The number of triangles increases by two each time.

   (C) The number of triangles increases by one each time.

   (D) The number of triangles increases by four each time.

4. How many triangles will be in the 15th shape?

   (F) 15

   (G) 20

   (H) 30

   (J) 35

5. What value does b have to be to make both equations true?

   $b - 7 = 15$; $2 \times 11 = b$

   (A) 85

   (B) 12

   (C) 21

   (D) 22

6. $(16 - 5)3 =$

   (F) 1

   (G) 33

   (H) 43

   (J) 45

DIRECTIONS: Choose the best answer. Use the bar graph for question 7.

Number of People Attending Basketball Games in January

7. How many more people attended the Jan. 6 game than the Jan. 12 game?

   (A) 10,000

   (B) 8,000

   (C) 5,000

   (D) 2,000

STOP

Mathematics

3.A

Defining Geometric Figures
Geometry

DIRECTIONS: Write the name of each polygon.

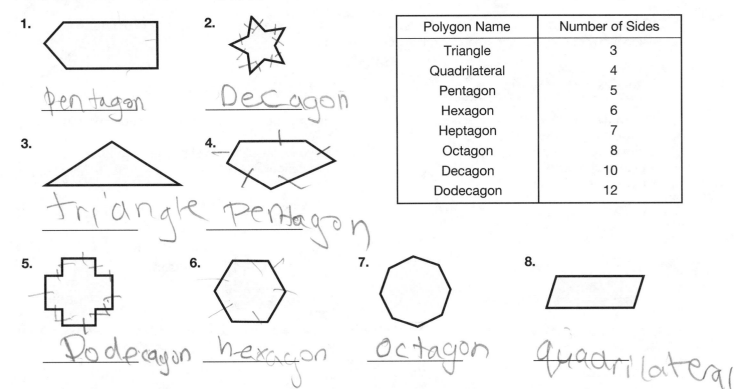

1. pentagon

2. Decagon

3. triangle

4. pentagon

Polygon Name	Number of Sides
Triangle	3
Quadrilateral	4
Pentagon	5
Hexagon	6
Heptagon	7
Octagon	8
Decagon	10
Dodecagon	12

5. Dodecagon

6. hexagon

7. octagon

8. quadrilateral

DIRECTIONS: Write the letter of the correct polygon name on the blank next to the matching shape.

Polygon Name

A. triangle

B. quadrilateral

C. pentagon

D. hexagon

E. heptagon

F. octagon

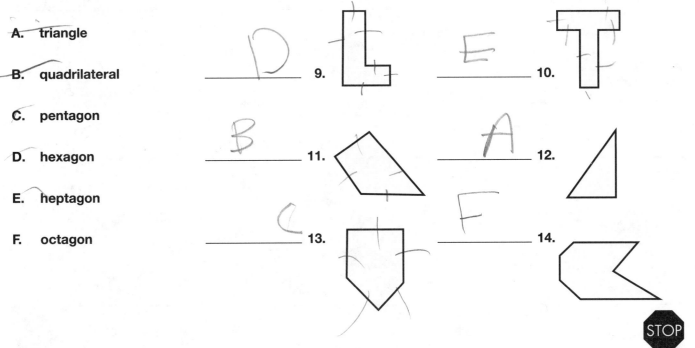

D ___ 9.

E ___ 10.

B ___ 11.

A ___ 12.

C ___ 13.

F ___ 14.

STOP

Identifying Pyramids and Prisms
Geometry

DIRECTIONS: Next to each shape below, write **prism, pyramid,** or **neither** to show what type of three-dimensional object it is. Be prepared to explain your choices.

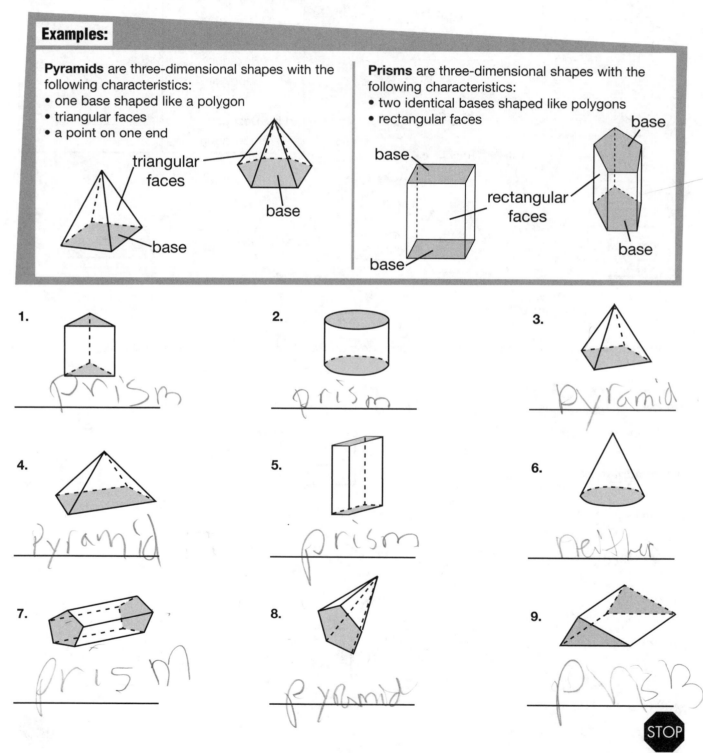

Examples:

Pyramids are three-dimensional shapes with the following characteristics:
• one base shaped like a polygon
• triangular faces
• a point on one end

triangular faces

base

Prisms are three-dimensional shapes with the following characteristics:
• two identical bases shaped like polygons
• rectangular faces

base

rectangular faces

base

base

1. _prism_

2. _prism_

3. _pyramid_

4. _pyramid_

5. _prism_

6. _neither_

7. _prism_

8. _pyramid_

9. _prism_

STOP

Mathematics

3.B

Describing Paths Using Coordinate Systems
Geometry

DIRECTIONS: Write the coordinate pairs for each figure plotted.

Clue Points on a graph are labeled using coordinate pairs. The first value in the pair represents the horizontal distance from zero. A positive number means to move right. A negative number means to move left. The second value in the pair represents the vertical distance from zero. A positive number means to move up. A negative number means to move down.

Look at the example point graphed on the grid below. This point is 5 units to the left of zero and 4 units above zero. Therefore, it would be labeled (−5, 4). The point (−5, 4) is called a **coordinate pair** or an **ordered pair**.

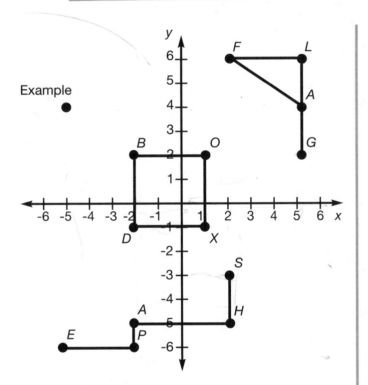

1. FLAG

$F = (2 , 6)$

$L = (5 , 6)$

$A = (5 , 4)$

$G = (5 , 2)$

2. BOXD

$B = (2, 2)$

$O = (1 , 1)$

$X = (1 , -1)$

$D = (-1 , -2)$

3. SHAPE

$S = (2 , -3)$

$H = (2 , -4)$

$A = (2 , -3)$

$P = (-2 , 6)$

$E = (5 , 6)$

DIRECTIONS: Find the best answer.

4. Look at the coordinate grid. Which sequence of ordered pairs would allow you to move from the school to the library?

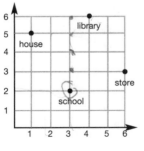

Ⓐ (2,3), (3,3), (4,3), (5,3), (6,3), (6,4)

Ⓑ (3,2), (3,3), (3,4), (3,5), (2,5), (1,5)

Ⓒ (3,2), (3,3), (3,4), (3,5), (3,6), (4,6)

Ⓓ (2,3), (2,4), (2,5), (2,6), (3,6), (4,6)

Mathematics

| 3.C |

Similar and Congruent
Geometry

DIRECTIONS: Measure the angles and sides of the shapes. Write **congruent** or **similar** below each set of shapes based on your findings.

Clue

Congruent shapes have the same measures of angles and sides.
Similar shapes have the same measures of angles, but not of sides.

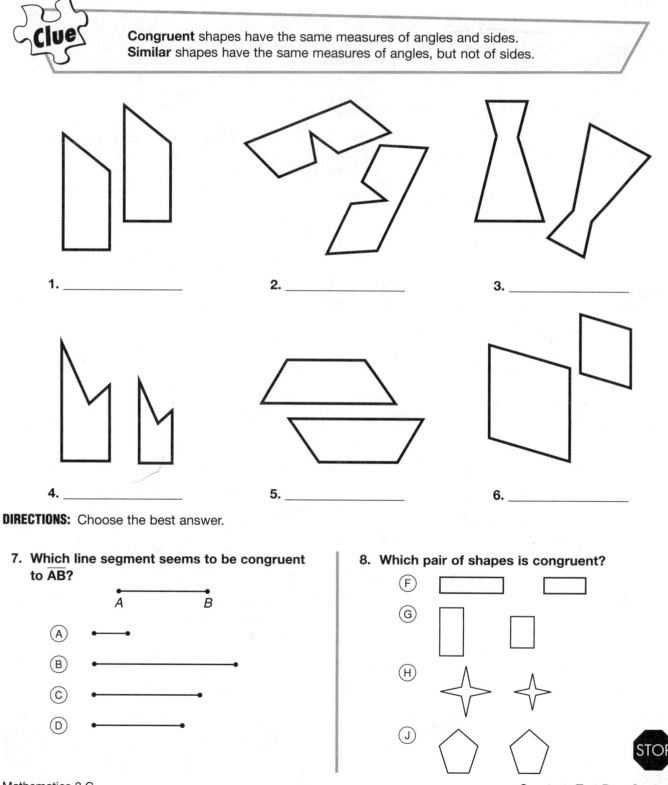

1. _____

2. _____

3. _____

4. _____

5. _____

6. _____

DIRECTIONS: Choose the best answer.

7. **Which line segment seems to be congruent to $\overline{AB}$?**

   A •——•

   B •————————•

   C •——————•

   D •——————•

8. **Which pair of shapes is congruent?**

   F

   G

   H

   J

STOP

Mathematics

3.D

Sketching Shapes
Geometry

DIRECTIONS: Name and draw the described polygon.

Clue | Before you choose an answer, ask yourself if the answer makes sense. If you are confused by a problem, read it again. If you are still confused, skip the problem and come back to it later.

1. **Polygon with three equal sides**

   Shape: _____

2. **Polygon with opposite sides equal and four right angles**

   Shape: _____

3. **Polygon with three sides of different lengths**

   Shape: _____

4. **Polygon with four sides equal, opposite sides parallel, and four angles equal**

   Shape: _____

5. **A three-dimensional shape with a polygon for a base and triangles with a common vertex**

   Shape: _____

6. **Completely curved three-dimensional shape**

   Shape: _____

Matching Views of
Three-Dimensional Models
Geometry

DIRECTIONS: Choose the best answer.

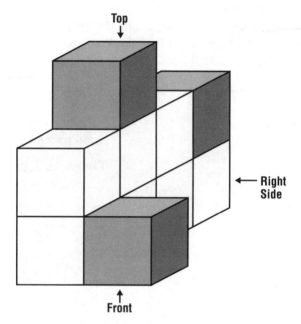

Top ↓

← Right Side

↑ Front

1. Which of these shows the right side view of the figure above?

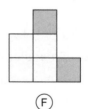

Ⓐ   Ⓑ   Ⓒ   Ⓓ

2. Which of these shows the front view of the figure above?

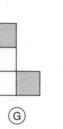   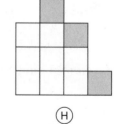   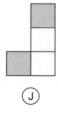

Ⓕ   Ⓖ   Ⓗ   Ⓙ

3. Which of these shows the top view of the figure above?

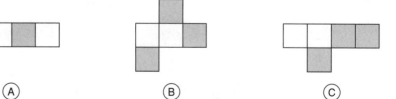

Ⓐ   Ⓑ   Ⓒ   Ⓓ

STOP

Name _____ Date _____

4.A

Equivalent Metric Measures
Measurement

DIRECTIONS: The metric system is based on multiples of 10. Use the following metric conversion charts to help you answer questions 1–20.

Metric Units of Length	Metric Units of Capacity	Metric Units of Mass
1 centimeter (cm) = 10 millimeters (mm)	1 liter (L) = 1,000 milliliters (mL)	1 gram (g) = 1,000 milligrams (mg)
1 meter (m) = 100 centimeters (cm)	1 decaliter (daL) = 10 liters (L)	1 kilogram (kg) = 1,000 grams (g)
1 kilometer (km) = 1,000 meters (m)	1 hectoliter (hL) = 100 liters (L)	1 decagram (dag) = 10 grams (g)
	1 kiloliter (kL) = 1,000 liters (L)	1 hectogram (hg) = 100 grams (g)
		1 metric ton (t) = 1,000 kilograms (kg)

1. Jesse measured her computer screen. It was 40 centimeters wide. How many millimeters is this? _____

2. Devon has a container that is 24 centimeters long. He found an item that is 186 millimeters long. Will it fit in the container? _____

3. Kayla climbed 2.5 meters up a ladder. How many centimeters is this? _____

4. Jackson's art project is 45 centimeters by 90 centimeters. Will it fit into a box that is .5 meter by 1 meter? _____

5. Kenny's book is 30 millimeters thick. How many centimeters thick is the book?
   - (A) 0.3 cm
   - (B) 3 cm
   - (C) 33 cm
   - (D) 300 cm

6. Which of the following equals 2,000 meters?
   - (F) 200 km
   - (G) 0.2 km
   - (H) 20 km
   - (J) 2 km

7. 3,000 mL = _____ L

8. 4 daL = _____ L

9. 6 kL = _____ L

10. 10 kL = _____ daL

11. 25 hL = _____ daL

12. 700 mL = _____ L

13. 80 hL = _____ kL

14. 10 kg = _____ g

15. 1 hg = _____ dag

16. 2,000 g = _____ kg

17. 500 g = _____ kg

18. 70 hg = _____ kg

19. 2 g = _____ mg

20. 3 t = _____ kg

Mathematics

| 4.A |

Approximate Measurements
Measurement

DIRECTIONS: Draw a line from the description on the left to the approximate length on the right.

1. length of a pen   .25 mile

2. length of a paper clip   20,000 feet

3. one lap on a track surrounding a football field   13 centimeters

4. length of a car   1.25 inches

5. elevation of the tallest mountain in Alaska   4 meters

DIRECTIONS: Choose the best answer.

6. A hot dog weighs _____ .
   - (A) a few pounds
   - (B) a few ounces
   - (C) a few grams
   - (D) a few milligrams

7. Lucinda wants to run in the newly created Fort Worth 10,000. It is a 10,000 meter race. The farthest Lucinda has ever run before is 1/2 that distance. In kilometers, what is the greatest distance Lucinda has ever run before?
   - (F) 5 km
   - (G) 10 km
   - (H) 50 km
   - (J) 1,000 km

8. This fingernail is about 1 centimeter wide. About how many centimeters long is this paper clip?

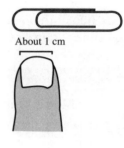
About 1 cm

   - (A) 1 cm
   - (B) 2 cm
   - (C) 3 cm
   - (D) 4 cm

9. Which measurement is about the same as the length of a baseball bat?
   - (F) 1 meter
   - (G) 1 kilometer
   - (H) 1 centimeter
   - (J) 1 millimeter

10. About how long is a city block?
   - (A) 120 meters
   - (B) 55 centimeters
   - (C) 48 kilometers
   - (D) 100 millimeters

11. About how much does a loaf of bread weigh?
   - (F) 500 ounces
   - (G) 500 grams
   - (H) 500 milligrams
   - (J) 500 kilograms

STOP

Name _____ Date _____

Mathematics

Estimating Area
Measurement

DIRECTIONS: For each of the following figures, estimate the area of the shaded portion. Circle the number choice that is most likely the area (in square units) beneath each figure.

Example:

You can estimate the area of an irregular shape by looking at the squares around it. In the example on the right, you know that 4 full squares are covered, so the area will be greater than 4 square units. You also know that the total figure is not larger than 16 square units (4 units × 4 units). You can estimate the area of the figure is between 4 and 16 square units.

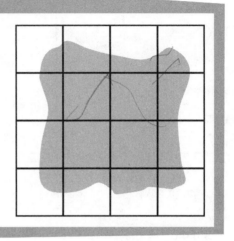

1.

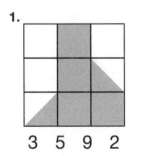

3   5   9   2

2.

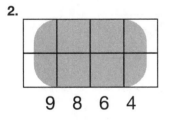

9   8   6   4

3.

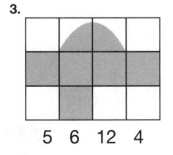

5   6   12   4

4.

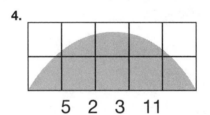

5   2   3   11

5.

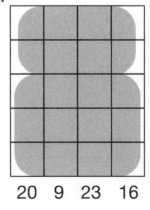

20   9   23   16

Mathematics
4.B

Area of Squares, Rectangles, and Right Triangles
Measurement

DIRECTIONS: Use the shapes below to develop the correct formulas.

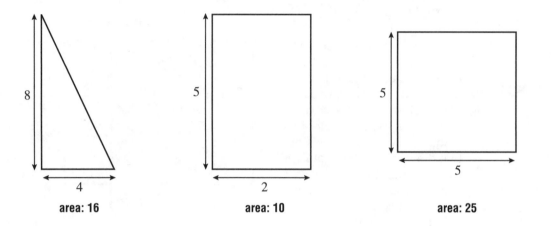

area: 16   area: 10   area: 25

1. **Which of the following is the correct formula for finding the area of a right triangle?**

   (A) base × height

   (B) $\frac{1}{2}$ base × height

   (C) base + height

   (D) $\frac{1}{2}$ base × $\frac{1}{2}$ height

2. **Which of the following is the correct formula for finding the area of a rectangle?**

   (F) (length × 2) + (width × 2)

   (G) length + width

   (H) length × width

   (J) length^2

3. **Which of the following is the correct formula for finding the area of a square?**

   (A) length^2

   (B) 4 × length

   (C) 2 × length

   (D) $\frac{1}{2}$ length × $\frac{1}{2}$ length

DIRECTIONS: Find the area of the following shapes.

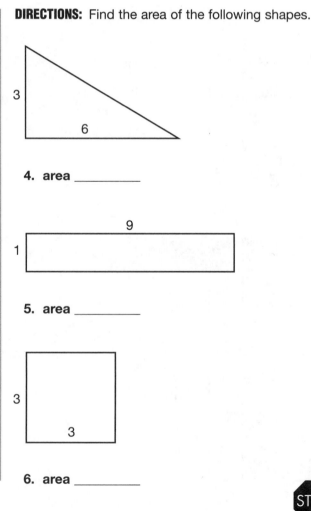

4. area _____

5. area _____

6. area _____

Mathematics

3.0–4.0

For pages 55–64

Mini-Test 2

Geometry; Measurement

DIRECTIONS: Choose the best answer.

1. Which of the figures below is a sphere?

(A)   (B)

(C)   (D)

2. Which of these shows the top view of the figure below?

(F)   (G)   (H)   (J)

3. A hair comb weighs about 35 grams. How many milligrams does that equal?

(A) 3.5

(B) 35,000

(C) 350

(D) 3,500

4. A rectangle has a length of 15 and a width of 5. What is the area?

(F) 20 square units

(G) 75 square units

(H) 3 square units

(J) 40 square units

5. Which line segment seems to be congruent to MN?

M   N

(A)

(B)

(C)

(D)

6. Which two shapes are congruent?

Figure A   Figure B   Figure C   Figure D

(F) A and B

(G) B and C

(H) B and D

(J) A and C

DIRECTIONS: Use this graph to answer question 7.

7. What point is at (5,8)?

(A) W

(B) X

(C) Y

(D) Z

STOP

Mathematics

5.A

Gathering and Communicating Data
Data Analysis and Probability

DIRECTIONS: Gina asked 250 students about their favorite types of restaurants. Her results are shown in the chart below. Use the chart to answer the questions.

Restaurant Type	Number
Italian	85
Bar & Grill	32
Mexican	45
Fast Food	70
Chinese	18

1. Each tick mark on the vertical axis in the chart below represents _____ people. Put a scale on the vertical axis.

2. Label the vertical axis.

3. What is the range of the data? _____

4. Complete the bar graph, using the data from the table.

Restaurant Preferences

| Italian | Bar & Grill | Mexican | Fast Food | Chinese |

5. How do you think Gina's data would have been different if she had asked people about their favorite restaurants as they were going into a local Italian diner? Explain.

_____

_____

Name _____ Date _____

 5.B

Finding the Mean
Data Analysis and Probability

DIRECTIONS: The fifth-grade class at Martin Luther King, Jr. Middle School collects items to donate to a local homeless shelter. The chart below shows an inventory of items collected. Use the chart to answer the questions.

Clue   The **mean**, or average, of a set of data is the sum of the data divided by the number of pieces of data.

Items	Last Year	This Year
Snack foods	21	32
Paper goods	28	42
Instant foods	22	38
Canned goods	42	63
Infant clothing	42	40

1. **Find the average number of items collected each year.**

   Last Year: _____ **This Year:** _____

2. **What was the difference in the mean number of items collected?** _____

3. **Which item showed the greatest increase from last year to this year?** _____
   Which items showed a decrease? _____

4. **Which year showed the most variation in the types of items collected? Explain.**

   _____

   _____

   _____

   _____

5. **Based on this data, what can the class predict will happen with the collection next year?**

   _____

   _____

   _____

   _____

   _____

   _____

   _____

Mathematics

| 5.C |

Making Predictions
Data Analysis and Probability

DIRECTIONS: Choose the best answer.

1. If all these chips were put into a bag, what is the probability that you would pick a chip with a letter that comes before M in the alphabet?

   (A) $\frac{3}{5}$

   (B) $\frac{3}{8}$

   (C) $\frac{5}{3}$

   (D) $\frac{5}{8}$

   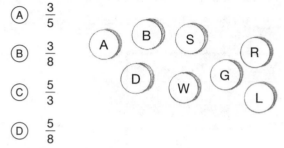

2. For the above chips, what is the probability that you would pick a chip with a vowel?

   (F) $\frac{1}{7}$

   (G) $\frac{1}{8}$

   (H) $\frac{7}{1}$

   (J) $\frac{8}{1}$

3. Which spinner would give you the best chance of landing on the number 2?

   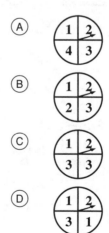

4. Which spinner would give you the best chance of landing on the number 4?

   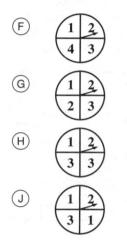

5. A bag of jelly beans contains 5 cherry jelly beans, 3 licorice jelly beans, 6 lime jelly beans, and 6 lemon jelly beans. When randomly pulling a jelly bean from the bag, which two colors are you equally likely to pick?

   (A) cherry and licorice

   (B) licorice and lime

   (C) lime and lemon

   (D) cherry and lime

6. Carol wants a cherry jelly bean. Without looking, she reaches into the bag and grabs a lime jelly bean. She puts the jelly bean back in the bag. Again, she randomly chooses a jelly bean. How does her chance of getting a cherry jelly bean on the second grab compare to her first grab?

   (F) better

   (G) worse

   (H) same

   (J) not here

Mathematics

5.D

Possible and Probable Outcomes
Data Analysis and Probability

DIRECTIONS: Choose the best answer.

Clue Choose "not here" only if you are sure the right answer is not one of the choices. Look for key words, numbers, and figures in each problem, and be sure you perform the correct operation.

1. There are 10 silver earrings and 10 gold earrings in a jewelry box. Cheryl reaches in without looking. What is the probability that she will pick a gold earring?

   Ⓐ $\frac{1}{2}$

   Ⓑ $\frac{1}{3}$

   Ⓒ $\frac{1}{4}$

   Ⓓ not here

2. A group of teachers are ordering sandwiches from the deli. They can choose ham, beef, turkey, or bologna on white bread, wheat bread, or rye bread. How many different meat and bread combinations are possible?

   Ⓕ 12

   Ⓖ 16

   Ⓗ 7

   Ⓙ not here

3. Elliott spun the arrow on a spinner 30 times. The results are shown in the table. Which of these spinners did Elliott most likely spin?

Diamond	Heart	Spade	Total Spins
11	10	9	30

   Ⓐ Ⓑ Ⓒ Ⓓ

4. A snack food company makes chewy fruit shapes of lions, monkeys, elephants, and giraffes in red, green, purple, and yellow. They put the same number of each kind in a package. How many different outcomes are there?

   Ⓕ 4

   Ⓖ 8

   Ⓗ 16

   Ⓙ not here

DIRECTIONS: For questions 5–7, write a **1** in the blank if the probability is certain; write a **0** if the probability is impossible; for other probabilities, write **NA**.

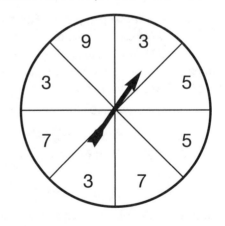

5. an even number? _____

6. a 3? _____

7. a number larger than 2? _____

Mathematics

| 6.A |

Solving Problems
Process

DIRECTIONS: Choose the best answer.

Clue You might find it helpful to use scratch paper to draw pictures or record information to solve many of these problems.

1. Two numbers have a product of 108 and a quotient of 12. What are the two numbers?

   (A) 9, 12

   (B) 7, 16

   (C) 36, 3

   (D) 54, 6

2. There are several uninvited ants at a picnic in the park. Among the 9 guests that are ants or people, there are 30 legs altogether. Each ant has 6 legs. How many ants are at the picnic?

   (F) 9 ants

   (G) 6 ants

   (H) 4 ants

   (J) 3 ants

3. Mr. Grace found three programs that he wanted to buy for the classroom. *Math Busters* was $21.80. *Spelling Practice* was $16.85. *Reading Classics* was $13.65. He spent a total of $35.45. What programs did he buy?

   (A) *Math Busters* and *Spelling Practice*

   (B) *Math Busters* and *Reading Classics*

   (C) *Spelling Practice* and *Reading Classics*

   (D) none of these

4. Carla has 6 hockey cards. Ed and Carla together have 16 hockey cards. Judith and Ed together have 25 hockey cards. How many hockey cards does Judith have?

   (F) 6 hockey cards

   (G) 9 hockey cards

   (H) 15 hockey cards

   (J) 20 hockey cards

5. The number of people watching a hockey game is 900 when rounded to the nearest hundred and 850 when rounded to the nearest ten. Which of these could be the number of people watching the game?

   (A) 847 people

   (B) 849 people

   (C) 856 people

   (D) 852 people

6. The Card Shop receives a shipment of trading cards each month. There are 8 hockey cards in a pack, 12 packs in a box, and 16 boxes in a shipping crate. Which is the total number of hockey cards in the shipping crate?

   (F) 1,536 hockey cards

   (G) 672 hockey cards

   (H) 1,436 hockey cards

   (J) 662 hockey cards

7. After the hockey game, each of these players bought a can of soda from a machine that takes both coins and bills. The soda costs 70¢ per can.

   Luke used only dimes.

   Jacques used only quarters.

   Pierre used only half-dollars.

   Roland used a dollar bill.

   Which two players got the same amount of change?

   (A) Luke and Jacques

   (B) Jacques and Pierre

   (C) Pierre and Roland

   (D) Roland and Luke

Name _____   Date _____

Mathematics

6.B/6.C

Developing
Mathematical Arguments
Process

DIRECTIONS: Choose the best answer.

1. Monica ate $\frac{1}{8}$ of her sandwich for lunch, Sam ate $\frac{2}{3}$ of his apple, and Rick drank all of his milk. How much of her milk did Monica drink?

   (A) $\frac{1}{8}$ of the milk

   (B) $\frac{2}{3}$ of the milk

   (C) all of the milk

   (D) not enough information

2. There were 258 cans of soup on the grocery store shelf in the morning. At 1:00 P.M., there were 156 cans of soup on the shelf. By the time the store closed at 7:00 P.M., several more cans of soup had been sold. How many cans of soup did the store sell in the entire day?

   (F) 102 cans

   (G) 288 cans

   (H) 414 cans

   (J) not enough information

3. Sasha went to the park at 9:30 A.M. She played for 45 minutes and then started soccer practice. She had soccer practice for 90 minutes. At what time did soccer practice end?

   (A) 10:45 A.M.

   (B) 11:15 A.M.

   (C) 11:45 A.M.

   (D) not enough information

4. Jessica must find the area of a square with one side that is 12 inches long. How can Jessica figure it out?

   (F) She can add all the sides together.

   (G) She can multiply 2 sides together.

   (H) She can divide 2 sides by each other.

   (J) She cannot figure out the area with the information she has.

5. Mavis works at the hardware store. Her hourly wage is $4.50. How much money is Mavis paid for one week's work? Which piece of information will help you solve this problem?

   (A) the number of hours she works each day

   (B) the number of days she works each week

   (C) the number of hours she works each week

   (D) the address of the hardware store

6. At the school store, José bought 2 pencils for $0.10 each, a notebook for $0.65, and a candy bar for $0.40. To find out how much change he will get, you need to know _____ .

   (F) how much 2 notebooks cost

   (G) how much money he gave the salesperson

   (H) how much he saved by buying one notebook

   (J) how much money he has

Name _____ Date _____

6.D # Using Mathematical Language
Process

DIRECTIONS: Choose the best answer.

Example:

The Florida State Fair is held every year in Tampa. At one of the state fairs, there were 48 Girl Scouts marching in the parade. There were 6 girls in each row. Which equation would you use to find how many rows of Girl Scouts were marching in the parade?

(A) $48 + 6 = n$ (C) $48 - n = 6$

(B) $n \times 6 = 48$ (D) $48 \times 6 = n$

Answer: (B)

---

1. A factory has 314 workers. The owner gave a total bonus of $612,300. Which number sentence shows how to find the amount of bonus money each worker received? Let b = amount of bonus money.

(A) $b + 314 = \$612,300$

(B) $b \times 314 = \$612,300$

(C) $b - 314 = \$612,300$

(D) $b \div 314 = \$612,300$

2. The human heart pumps about 24 liters of blood in 5 minutes. You want to know about how many liters of blood are pumped in 1 minute. Which math problem will help you find the answer?

(F) $24 \div 5 = \blacksquare$

(G) $24 \times 5 = \blacksquare$

(H) $24 + 5 = \blacksquare$

(J) $24 - 5 = \blacksquare$

3. A flea can jump 130 times its own height. If you could do the same thing, and your height is 54 inches, how high could you jump? Which math problem could help you find the answer?

(A) $130 + 54 = \blacksquare$

(B) $130 - 54 = \blacksquare$

(C) $130 \div 54 = \blacksquare$

(D) $130 \times 54 = \blacksquare$

4. Joyce collects football cards. She puts them into stacks of 9 cards each. She has 36 stacks of cards. She wants to know how many cards she has in all. Which computation shows how to find the correct answer?

(F) $36 + 9 = 45$

(G) $36 \times 9 = 324$

(H) $36 \div 9 = 4$

(J) $36 - 9 = 27$

5. LaToya has 72 books in her collection. She wants to put only 8 books on each of her shelves. Which expression could she use to figure out how many shelves she will need for her books?

(A) $72 + 8 = s$

(B) $72 - 8 = s$

(C) $72 \div 8 = s$

(D) $s \div 8 = 72$

6. Marlo drove 350 miles in 7 hours and used 17.5 gallons of gas. How do you determine her speed?

(F) $350 \times 7 \div 17.5$

(G) $350 \div 17.5$

(H) 17.5×7

(J) $350 \div 7$

Name _____ Date _____

Mathematics
| 6.E |
Using Pictures and Models
Process

DIRECTIONS: Choose the best answer.

1. Which figure below is $\frac{4}{9}$ shaded?

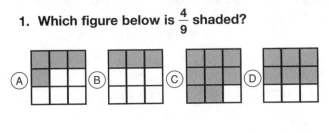

2. The length of *YZ* is what fraction of the length of *VX*?

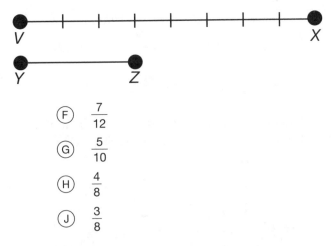

    (F) $\frac{7}{12}$

    (G) $\frac{5}{10}$

    (H) $\frac{4}{8}$

    (J) $\frac{3}{8}$

3. Tenisha made a number chart on which she shaded all the multiples of 5. Which pattern shows the shading on her number chart?

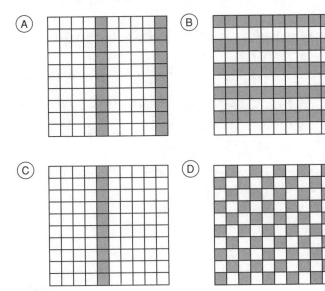

4. Which number tells how much of this group of shapes is shaded?

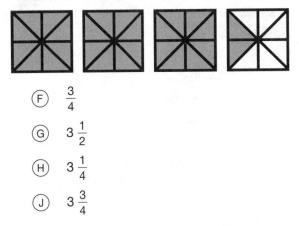

    (F) $\frac{3}{4}$

    (G) $3\frac{1}{2}$

    (H) $3\frac{1}{4}$

    (J) $3\frac{3}{4}$

DIRECTIONS: Use the pictograph below for number 5.

Number of Students at Highview School

Grade Level	Number of Students
Kindergarten	↟↟↟↟↟↟↟↟
1st Grade	↟↟↟↟↟↟↟↟↟↟↟↟
2nd Grade	↟↟↟↟↟↟↟
3rd Grade	↟↟↟↟↟↟↟↟
4th Grade	↟↟↟↟↟↟↟↟↟↟↟↟
5th Grade	↟↟↟↟↟↟↟

Key: ↟ = 5 students

5. How many Highview students are fifth graders?

    (A)   30 students

    (B)   35 students

    (C)   40 students

    (D)   60 students

Mathematics

5.0–6.0

For pages 66–73

Mini-Test 3

Data Analysis and Probability; Process

DIRECTIONS: Choose the best answer.

1. **Clarissa was paid $204 for 3 days of work. She worked 8 hours each day. What was her rate?**

   (A) $8.50 per hour

   (B) $8.50 per day

   (C) $25.50 per day

   (D) $68 per hour

2. **Which computation shows how to find the correct answer for question 1?**

   (F) 204 ÷ 3

   (G) 204 ÷ 8

   (H) (204 ÷ 3) × 8

   (J) 204 ÷ (3 × 8)

3. **If each** ☺ **stands for 3 people, how would you show 12 people?**

   (D) none of these

4. **What is the mean of this data?**

   31, 54, 34, 31, 56

   (F) 31

   (G) 34

   (H) 41.2

   (J) 51.5

DIRECTIONS: Use the following information for question 5. A bag contains 7 red marbles, 5 green marbles, 3 white marbles, and 2 gold marbles.

5. **If you reach into the bag without looking, what is the probability of picking a red marble?**

   (A) $\frac{7}{10}$

   (B) $\frac{7}{17}$

   (C) $\frac{7}{8}$

   (D) $\frac{7}{9}$

DIRECTIONS: The graph below shows the cost of a ticket to the movies in five different cities. Use the graph for question 6.

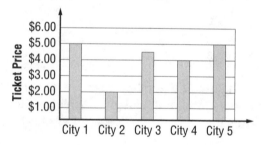

6. **Which cities have the same ticket price?**

   (F) Cities 1 and 3

   (G) Cities 3 and 5

   (H) Cities 1 and 5

   (J) Cities 4 and 5

How Am I Doing?

Mini-Test 1

Page 54

Number Correct

7 answers correct	**Great Job!** Move on to the section test on page 76.
5–6 answers correct	**You're almost there!** But you still need a little practice. Review practice pages 45–53 before moving on to the section test on page 76.
0–4 answers correct	**Oops!** Time to review what you have learned and try again. Review the practice section on pages 45–53. Then, retake the test on page 54. Now, move on to the section test on page 76.

Mini-Test 2

Page 65

Number Correct

7 answers correct	**Awesome!** Move on to the section test on page 76.
5–6 answers correct	**You're almost there!** But you still need a little practice. Review practice pages 55–64 before moving on to the section test on page 76.
0–4 answers correct	**Oops!** Time to review what you have learned and try again. Review the practice section on pages 55–64. Then, retake the test on page 65. Now, move on to the section test on page 76.

Mini-Test 3

Page 74

Number Correct

6 answers correct	**Great Job!** Move on to the section test on page 76.
3–5 answers correct	**You're almost there!** But you still need a little practice. Review practice pages 66–73 before moving on to the section test on page 76.
0–2 answers correct	**Oops!** Time to review what you have learned and try again. Review the practice section on pages 66–73. Then, retake the test on page 74. Now, move on to the section test on page 76.

Final Mathematics Test
for pages 45–73

DIRECTIONS: Choose the best answer.

1. **Which of the following is not equivalent to the shaded portion of the figure?**

   (A) $\frac{1}{3}$

   (B) $\frac{4}{8}$

   (C) $\frac{12}{36}$

   (D) $\frac{37}{111}$

   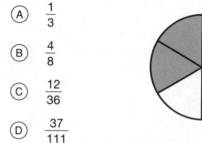

2. **It took Scott $\frac{3}{6}$ of an hour to get home. What is the decimal equivalent of $\frac{3}{6}$?**

   (F) 0.5

   (G) 0.36

   (H) 2.0

   (J) not here

3. **Each column in the number pattern below equals 21. What numbers are missing?**

3	5	2	1	6
2	7	8	9	1
9	8	4	6	7
	1	7		7

   (A) 6 and 8

   (B) 7 and 5

   (C) 1 and 7

   (D) 4 and 3

4. **Which of these rules is correct?**

   (F) Half of any even number is odd.

   (G) Half of any even number is even.

   (H) All odd numbers can be divided by 3.

   (J) All even numbers can be divided by 2.

5. **Jaime read for 30 minutes on Monday, 47 minutes on Tuesday, 64 minutes on Wednesday, and 81 minutes on Thursday. Which statement describes Jaime's pattern for reading?**

   (A) Add 15 minutes each day.

   (B) Subtract 17 minutes each day.

   (C) Add 12 minutes each day.

   (D) Add 17 minutes each day.

DIRECTIONS: A survey on favorite colors was taken at Rosa's school. The graph below shows the results of the survey. Study the graph, then answer questions 6 and 7.

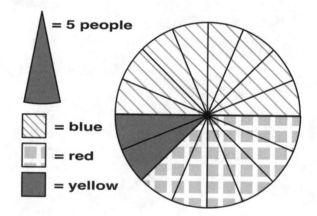

= 5 people

= blue

= red

= yellow

6. **How many more students prefer the color red over yellow?**

   (F) 4

   (G) 12

   (H) 20

   (J) 35

7. **How many students chose blue as their favorite color?**

   (A) 8

   (B) 50

   (C) 24

   (D) 40

GO

DIRECTIONS: Use the graph for question 8.

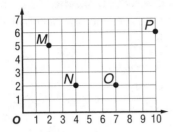

8. In the graph above, which point is located at (4, 2)?

   F) *P*

   G) *O*

   H) *N*

   J) *M*

DIRECTIONS: Choose the best answer.

9. Jeremiah has a photograph that measures 5" × 7". He wants to frame the photograph using a 3-inch mat. What size picture frame will Jeremiah need to accommodate the photograph and mat?

   A) 5" × 7"

   B) 8" × 10"

   C) 3" × 5"

   D) 11" × 13"

10. A football is 11 inches in length. How many footballs would have to be placed end to end to equal more than 1 yard?

    F) 1

    G) 2

    H) 3

    J) 4

11. In which of these is *y* equal to 9?

    A) $17 \div 8 = y$

    B) $y + 17 = 8$

    C) $y + 8 = 17$

    D) $8 \times y = 17$

12. Which of the figures below are congruent?

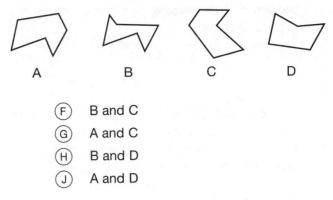

    F) B and C

    G) A and C

    H) B and D

    J) A and D

13. What is the approximate area of this shape?

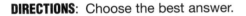

    A) 16 square units

    B) 18 square units

    C) 20 square units

    D) 23 square units

14. What is the area of this rectangle?

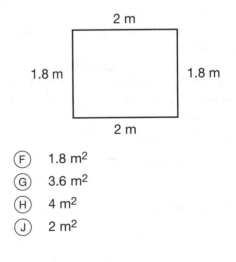

    F) 1.8 m²

    G) 3.6 m²

    H) 4 m²

    J) 2 m²

15. Timmy flips a coin 10 times and gets 8 heads and 2 tails. What would he expect the next flip to result in?

    Ⓐ   heads

    Ⓑ   tails

16. On a baseball diamond, it is 90 feet between each base, and there are four bases. Suppose a runner hits a double and has reached second base. How much farther does the runner have to go to reach home?

    Ⓕ   90 ft.

    Ⓖ   180 ft.

    Ⓗ   270 ft.

    Ⓙ   360 ft.

17. The Spanish Club wants to buy a set of instructional videos. Each video costs $12.50. What information will they need to determine how much money they must raise to buy the entire set of videos?

    Ⓐ   the number of students in the school

    Ⓑ   how long each video is

    Ⓒ   the number of videos in the set

    Ⓓ   how many students there are in the Spanish Club

18. Natasha is building her strength for the swimming season. She can now lift 75 pounds. She wants to increase the weight she can lift by 5 pounds a week for 6 weeks. At the end of 6 weeks, how much weight should she be able to lift?

    Ⓕ   105 pounds

    Ⓖ   30 pounds

    Ⓗ   92 pounds

    Ⓙ   80 pounds

19. An auto mechanic earns $19 an hour. She works 8 hours a day. Which number sentence shows how to find how much she earns in a day?

    Ⓐ $19 + 8 = \blacksquare$

    Ⓑ $19 - 8 = \blacksquare$

    Ⓒ $19 \times 8 = \blacksquare$

    Ⓓ $19 \div 8 = \blacksquare$

20. What value does b have to be to make both equations true?

$$b - 9 = 15; 2 \times 12 = b$$

    Ⓕ   22

    Ⓖ   23

    Ⓗ   24

    Ⓙ   30

21. Which of the following equals 27 cm?

    Ⓐ   270 mm

    Ⓑ   2.7 m

    Ⓒ   270 m

    Ⓓ   2.7 mm

22. A three-dimensional figure with rectangular faces and two identical bases shaped like polygons is a

    Ⓕ   pyramid

    Ⓖ   sphere

    Ⓗ   cylinder

    Ⓙ   prism

23. A bag contains 10 nickels, 7 dimes, and 5 quarters. If you reach into the bag and take out one coin, what is the probability that you will take a nickel?

    Ⓐ $\dfrac{5}{11}$

    Ⓑ $\dfrac{5}{22}$

    Ⓒ $\dfrac{10}{12}$

    Ⓓ $\dfrac{10}{23}$

Mathematics Test

Answer Sheet

1 Ⓐ Ⓑ Ⓒ Ⓓ
2 Ⓕ Ⓖ Ⓗ Ⓙ
3 Ⓐ Ⓑ Ⓒ Ⓓ
4 Ⓕ Ⓖ Ⓗ Ⓙ
5 Ⓐ Ⓑ Ⓒ Ⓓ
6 Ⓕ Ⓖ Ⓗ Ⓙ
7 Ⓐ Ⓑ Ⓒ Ⓓ
8 Ⓕ Ⓖ Ⓗ Ⓙ
9 Ⓐ Ⓑ Ⓒ Ⓓ
10 Ⓕ Ⓖ Ⓗ Ⓙ

11 Ⓐ Ⓑ Ⓒ Ⓓ
12 Ⓕ Ⓖ Ⓗ Ⓙ
13 Ⓐ Ⓑ Ⓒ Ⓓ
14 Ⓕ Ⓖ Ⓗ Ⓙ
15 Ⓐ Ⓑ Ⓒ Ⓓ
16 Ⓕ Ⓖ Ⓗ Ⓙ
17 Ⓐ Ⓑ Ⓒ Ⓓ
18 Ⓕ Ⓖ Ⓗ Ⓙ
19 Ⓐ Ⓑ Ⓒ Ⓓ
20 Ⓕ Ⓖ Ⓗ Ⓙ

21 Ⓐ Ⓑ Ⓒ Ⓓ
22 Ⓕ Ⓖ Ⓗ Ⓙ
23 Ⓐ Ⓑ Ⓒ Ⓓ

Social Studies Standards

Standard 1—Culture *(See pages 81–82.)*
Social studies programs should include experiences that provide for the study of culture and cultural diversity.

Standard 2—Time, Continuity, and Change *(See pages 83–85.)*
Social studies programs should include experiences that provide for the study of the way human beings view themselves in and over time.

Standard 3—People, Places, and Environments *(See pages 86–88.)*
Social studies programs should include experiences that provide for the study of people, places, and environments.

Standard 4—Individual Development and Identity *(See pages 90–91.)*
Social studies programs should include experiences that provide for the study of individual development and identity.

Standard 5—Individuals, Groups, and Institutions *(See pages 92–93.)*
Social studies programs should include experiences that provide for the study of individuals, groups, and institutions.

Standard 6—Power, Authority, and Governance *(See pages 95–96.)*
Social studies programs should include experiences that provide for the study of how people create and change structures of power, authority, and governance.

Standard 7—Production, Distribution, and Consumption *(See pages 97–98.)*
Social studies programs should include experiences that provide for the study of how people organize for the production, distribution, and consumption of goods and services.

Standard 8—Science, Technology, and Society *(See page 99.)*
Social studies programs should include experiences that provide for the study of relationships among science, technology, and society.

Standard 9—Global Connections *(See pages 101–102.)*
Social studies programs should include experiences that provide for the study of global connections and interdependence.

Standard 10—Civic Ideals and Practices *(See pages 103–104.)*
Social studies programs should include experiences that provide for the study of the ideals, principles, and practices of citizenship in a democratic republic.

Name _____   Date _____

Comparing Ways Cultures Meet Needs
Culture

DIRECTIONS: Use the chart below to help you choose the best answer.

Native American Group	Where They Lived	Sources of Food	Kinds of Homes
Iroquois	Eastern Woodlands in eastern United States	Corn, squash, beans, deer, turkeys, geese, squirrel	Longhouses made of bark
Sioux	Great Plains in central United States	Buffalo	Tepees made from buffalo hides
Pueblo	Southwestern United States	Corn, beans, squash, turkeys	Homes of adobe and rocks
Chinook	Northwest coast of the United States	Fish	Wooden houses

1. **Which of the following best describes the way the Sioux met their needs?**

   Ⓐ They depended on trees for shelter.

   Ⓑ They farmed for all their food.

   Ⓒ They depended on the buffalo for food and shelter.

   Ⓓ They fished for all their food.

2. **Which of the following best describes how the Chinook met their needs?**

   Ⓕ They depended on the buffalo for food and shelter.

   Ⓖ They used mud and rock for their shelter.

   Ⓗ They depended only on farming for their food.

   Ⓙ They used resources from the ocean and forests.

3. **How did the Iroquois meet their need for food and shelter?**

   Ⓐ They used resources from the forest.

   Ⓑ They depended on the ocean for food.

   Ⓒ They depended on the buffalo for food and shelter.

   Ⓓ They made homes from clay.

4. **Based on the chart above, which of the following statements is true?**

   Ⓕ Native American groups built different kinds of homes, but they all ate the same kinds of food.

   Ⓖ Native American groups ate different kinds of food, but they built similar kinds of homes.

   Ⓗ All Native American groups needed food and shelter, but they met these needs in different ways.

   Ⓙ All Native American groups met their needs in the same way.

Name _____ Date _____

Social Studies

Transmission of Culture Through Celebrations
Culture

DIRECTIONS: Choose the best answer.

1. **This holiday is celebrated in the United States, Canada, and most Latin American nations to honor working men and women.**
   - (A) Labor Day
   - (B) Independence Day
   - (C) President's Day
   - (D) Thanksgiving Day

2. **This Mexican national holiday honors the Mexican victory over the French army at Puebla de los Angeles on May 5, 1862.**
   - (F) Thanksgiving Day
   - (G) Election Day
   - (H) Cinco de Mayo
   - (J) St. Patrick's Day

3. **The founding of the city of Rio de Janeiro is celebrated on January 20 in parts of**
   _____ .
   - (A) Manitoba
   - (B) Brazil
   - (C) California
   - (D) New York

4. **The signing of the Declaration of Independence is celebrated in the United States on _____ .**
   - (F) the first Tuesday in November
   - (G) July 4
   - (H) January 1
   - (J) the fourth Thursday in November

5. **On Remembrance Day, Canadians honor those who have died while serving in the armed forces. It is observed on November 11. The American equivalent to Remembrance Day is observed on the last Monday in May and is called _____ .**
   - (A) Memorial Day
   - (B) Flag Day
   - (C) President's Day
   - (D) Victoria Day

6. **Christopher Columbus's "discovery" of the New World is celebrated in many Latin American countries on _____ .**
   - (F) January 1
   - (G) February 14
   - (H) October 12
   - (J) December 25

DIRECTIONS: Read the passage below to answer question 7.

Simon Bolivar was one of South America's greatest statesmen, writers, and generals. His victories over Spain won independence for six nations—Bolivia, Panama, Colombia, Ecuador, Peru, and Venezuela. He is often referred to as "The Liberator" and the "George Washington of South America." He motivated thousands to fight and die for liberty.

7. **Two South American nations celebrate July 24 as Birth of the Liberator Day, or Simon Bolivar Day. Based on the passage, the two countries are probably _____ .**
   - (A) Brazil and Paraguay
   - (B) Peru and Cuba
   - (C) Chile and Uruguay
   - (D) Venezuela and Ecuador

Social Studies

2.0

Comparing Different Views of the Same Event
Time, Continuity, and Change

DIRECTIONS: Read the passages concerning the American Revolution and answer the questions on the following page.

Views of a twentieth-century historian:

American colonists had no elected representatives in the British Parliament. Therefore, the British government had no right to tax the colonies. They tried to raise money in 1765 by requiring a tax stamp on colonial documents, newspapers, and other printed papers. Colonists' opposition to the Stamp Act was justified. The colonial leaders who organized the Stamp Act Congress were right. Colonists could not be taxed without being represented in Parliament. The Stamp Act obviously weakened the colonists' rights and liberties.

Views of Samuel Johnson, an English writer who lived at the time of the American Revolution:

As man can be in but one place, at once, he cannot have the advantages of multiplied residence. He that will enjoy the brightness of sunshine, must quit the coolness of the shade. He who goes voluntarily to America, cannot complain of losing what he leaves in Europe. He, perhaps, had a right to vote for a knight or burgess; by crossing the Atlantick [sic], he has not nullified his right; but he has made its exertion no longer possible. By his own choice he has left a country, where he had a vote and little property, for another, where he has great property, but no vote.

Note: Source of second passage is *The Works of Samuel Johnson,* published by Pafraets & Company, Troy, New York, 1913; volume 14, pages 93–144.

British Policies Toward American Colonies

Policy	Description
Sugar Act	Lowered the tax on British molasses to stop the smuggling of sugar; set up courts to hear smuggling cases
Currency Act	Banned the use of paper money in the colonies
Stamp Act	Placed a tax on most printed materials
Quartering Act	Required colonists to provide barracks for or otherwise house British troops
Townshend Acts	Placed a tax on imported goods
Tea Act	Allowed a British tea company to sell directly to shopkeepers, bypassing colonial merchants who usually distributed imported tea
Declaratory Act	Declared that colonies were under the authority of the British Parliament, which had the power to make laws for the colonies
Coercive Acts	Closed Boston Harbor, banned town meetings and cancelled many elections, protected British soldiers from trials by colonists, and forced colonists to house British soldiers in their homes

GO

Name _____ Date _____

> **From the Declaration of Independence:**
>
> When in the Course of human events, it becomes necessary for one people to dissolve the political bands which have connected them with another, and to assume . . . the separate and equal station to which the Laws of Nature and of Nature's God entitle them . . . they should declare the causes which impel [force] them to the separation. . . .
>
> Governments are instituted among Men, deriving their just powers from the consent of the governed. . . .
>
> The history of the present King of Great Britain is a history of repeated injuries and usurpations [takings], all having in direct object the establishment of an absolute Tyranny over these States. . . .

1. **The historian's main point is that _____.**

   (A) colonists should never have to pay any taxes of any kind

   (B) colonists should not be taxed by the British because they could not vote in British elections

   (C) the British have every right to tax their colonies

   (D) all taxes are unlawful

2. **Samuel Johnson's main point is that**

   _____ .

   (F) whatever the colonists want is acceptable

   (G) the colonists should be taxed even more heavily

   (H) colonists have no right to complain about losing their vote in British elections

   (J) the British Army should arrest all colonists who refuse to pay their taxes

3. **Imagine that you are a British subject living in London in the 1760s. Explain why you think your government's policies toward the colonies are fair and just.**

   _____

   _____

   _____

   _____

   _____

4. **Do you think the American Revolution could have been avoided had the British government cancelled the policies to which the colonists objected? Or would the colonists eventually have insisted upon their independence no matter what the British government did? Defend your answer.**

   _____

   _____

   _____

   _____

   _____

Name _____ Date _____

Interpreting Events on a Time Line
Time, Continuity, and Change

DIRECTIONS: Use this time line to answer the questions about the Internet.

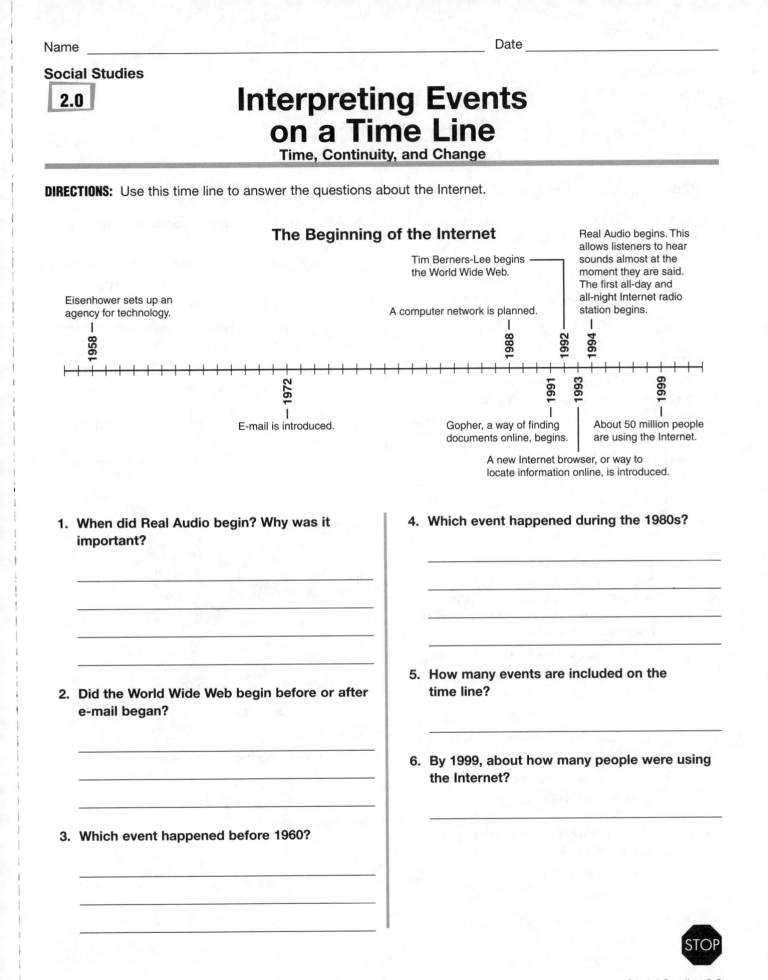

The Beginning of the Internet

Eisenhower sets up an agency for technology.
1958

1972
E-mail is introduced.

A computer network is planned.
1988

Tim Berners-Lee begins the World Wide Web.
1992

Real Audio begins. This allows listeners to hear sounds almost at the moment they are said. The first all-day and all-night Internet radio station begins.
1994

1991
Gopher, a way of finding documents online, begins.

1993
A new Internet browser, or way to locate information online, is introduced.

1999
About 50 million people are using the Internet.

1. **When did Real Audio begin? Why was it important?**

_____

_____

_____

_____

2. **Did the World Wide Web begin before or after e-mail began?**

_____

_____

3. **Which event happened before 1960?**

_____

_____

4. **Which event happened during the 1980s?**

_____

_____

_____

_____

5. **How many events are included on the time line?**

_____

6. **By 1999, about how many people were using the Internet?**

_____

_____

STOP

Name _____   Date _____

Geographic Factors and Society
People, Places, and Environments

DIRECTIONS: Choose the best answer.

1. Which of the following is not a reason people sometimes choose to live in mountainous areas?

   (A) protection from neighbors

   (B) frequent landslides

   (C) lots of tree-covered land

   (D) abundant wildlife

2. Over the past few decades, many Middle Eastern countries have quickly gone from very poor to very wealthy. Which resource is most responsible for this economic growth?

   (F) exotic fruits

   (G) oil

   (H) coffee

   (J) camels

3. Ships carry about 80 percent of all international cargo from one country to another. How might this fact affect the economic activities of a country that had no port or access to the ocean?

   (A) The country would have a more difficult time trading with other countries.

   (B) The country would probably be the richest one in the region.

   (C) The country's economic activities would be limited to farms and livestock.

   (D) The country would not be able to receive any supplies.

4. Where do you think the great majority of people on Earth live?

   (F) in forests

   (G) in deserts

   (H) in mountainous regions

   (J) along the coasts of oceans and lakes and along river valleys

5. Which of the following places will probably attract the most settlers?

   (A) A region surrounding a very polluted lake.

   (B) A region where the only crop that grows well is rutabagas.

   (C) A region where temperatures reach well below zero most of the time.

   (D) A mild region with fertile land where many crops grow well.

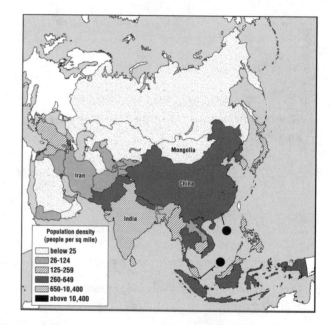

6. Based on the map above, which Asian country is the most crowded?

   (F) India

   (G) Mongolia

   (H) China

   (J) Iran

Name _____ Date _____

Effect of Natural Events on Human Activities
People, Places, and Environments

DIRECTIONS: Choose the best answer.

1. This spring, your neighbor's yard was full of dandelions; your yard had none. Next spring, you will find that you need to start weeding dandelions from your yard, too. Which of the following is probably most responsible for this situation?

   Ⓐ the amount of rain that falls in your area next spring

   Ⓑ the type of soil that is in your yard

   Ⓒ the average temperature next spring

   Ⓓ the wind carrying dandelion seeds to other areas

Characteristics of the Tundra
There is less than 25 cm annual rainfall
The winters are six to nine months long
The average temperature is −12°C
Only the top portion of the soil thaws during the short, cold summer
The soil is not fertile and does not support many plants

2. The physical environment of the tundra
   _____ .

   Ⓕ guarantees that almost no farming will occur there

   Ⓖ makes it impossible for people to live there at all

   Ⓗ would make it a poor spot to go ice fishing

   Ⓙ all of the above are true

3. How does the physical environment of the tundra affect the clothes worn by the people who live there?

   Ⓐ The temperature requires people to dress very warmly.

   Ⓑ Lack of plant life means that animal skins are used extensively for clothing.

   Ⓒ both A and B

   Ⓓ neither A nor B

4. Earthen dams are sometimes covered with plants to provide stability and prevent them from washing away. Which types of plants should be used in such situations?

   Ⓕ a variety of plants that grow well in that particular environment

   Ⓖ tall trees with deep roots

   Ⓗ roses

   Ⓙ mosses and lichens

5. A certain area regularly floods at least twice every year. Tell how this might affect the way people live in this area.

   _____

   _____

   _____

   _____

6. Describe two ways natural events in the physical environment might affect the life of a farmer. Be specific.

   _____

   _____

   _____

   _____

Social Studies

| 3.0 |

Using Maps
People, Places, and Environments

DIRECTIONS: Use the map to help you choose the best answer.

Clue — The map key explains the symbols that are used on the map.

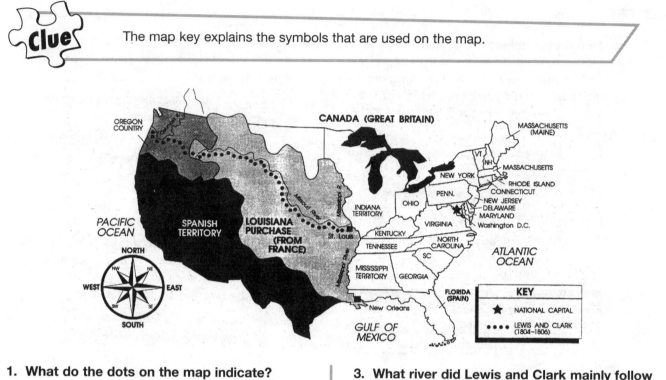

1. **What do the dots on the map indicate?**

   (A) the Missouri River

   (B) the border between the Louisiana territory and Canada

   (C) the route Lewis and Clark took during their expedition of the territory

   (D) the border between the land the U.S. purchased and the land still owned by France

2. **From whom did the United States buy the Louisiana Territory?**

   (F) France

   (G) Spain

   (H) Great Britain

   (J) Canada

3. **What river did Lewis and Clark mainly follow during their expedition?**

   (A) the Colorado River

   (B) the Columbia River

   (C) the Mississippi River

   (D) the Missouri River

4. **The Louisiana Purchase territory was _____ of the Mississippi River.**

   (F) north

   (G) south

   (H) east

   (J) west

5. **Which country controlled the land west of the Louisiana Purchase?**

   (A) Canada

   (B) Great Britain

   (C) Spain

   (D) the United States

Name _____   Date _____

Mini-Test 1

**Culture; Time, Continuity, and Change;
People, Places, and Environments**

DIRECTIONS: Study the time line below and answer questions 1–2.

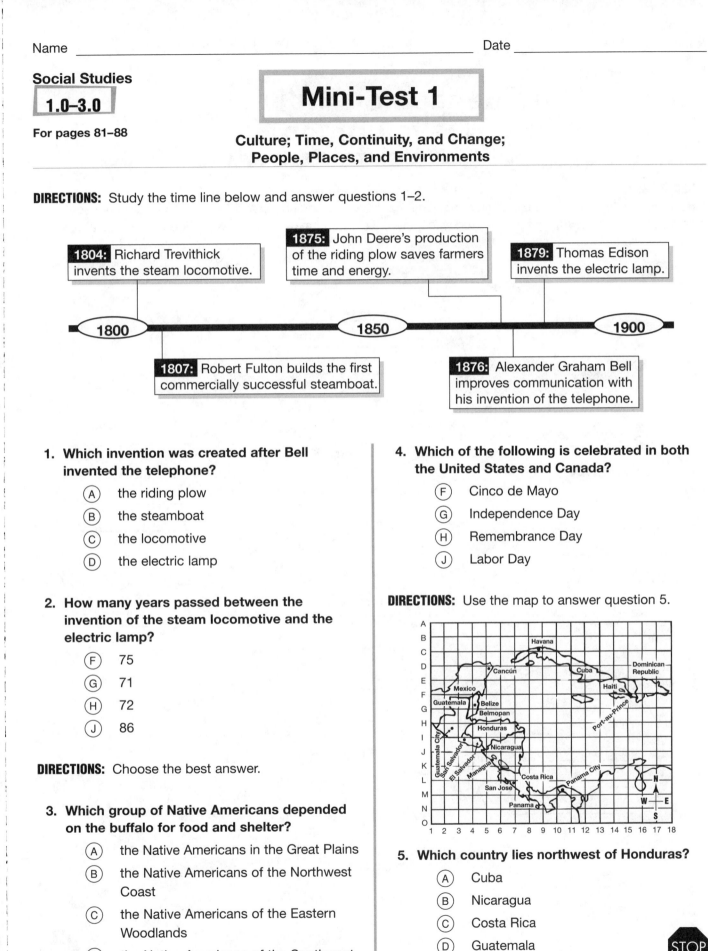

1804: Richard Trevithick invents the steam locomotive.

1875: John Deere's production of the riding plow saves farmers time and energy.

1879: Thomas Edison invents the electric lamp.

1800   **1850**   **1900**

1807: Robert Fulton builds the first commercially successful steamboat.

1876: Alexander Graham Bell improves communication with his invention of the telephone.

1. **Which invention was created after Bell invented the telephone?**

   Ⓐ the riding plow

   Ⓑ the steamboat

   Ⓒ the locomotive

   Ⓓ the electric lamp

2. **How many years passed between the invention of the steam locomotive and the electric lamp?**

   Ⓕ 75

   Ⓖ 71

   Ⓗ 72

   Ⓙ 86

DIRECTIONS: Choose the best answer.

3. **Which group of Native Americans depended on the buffalo for food and shelter?**

   Ⓐ the Native Americans in the Great Plains

   Ⓑ the Native Americans of the Northwest Coast

   Ⓒ the Native Americans of the Eastern Woodlands

   Ⓓ the Native Americans of the Southwest

4. **Which of the following is celebrated in both the United States and Canada?**

   Ⓕ Cinco de Mayo

   Ⓖ Independence Day

   Ⓗ Remembrance Day

   Ⓙ Labor Day

DIRECTIONS: Use the map to answer question 5.

5. **Which country lies northwest of Honduras?**

   Ⓐ Cuba

   Ⓑ Nicaragua

   Ⓒ Costa Rica

   Ⓓ Guatemala

STOP

Social Studies

| 4.0 |

Influences on Individual Development
Individual Development and Identity

DIRECTIONS: People are who they are because of many different factors. All of these factors help to make each person a unique individual. Think about what makes you a unique person. Then, in the diagram below, give an example of how your family, heredity, culture, friends, and experiences have helped make you a unique individual.

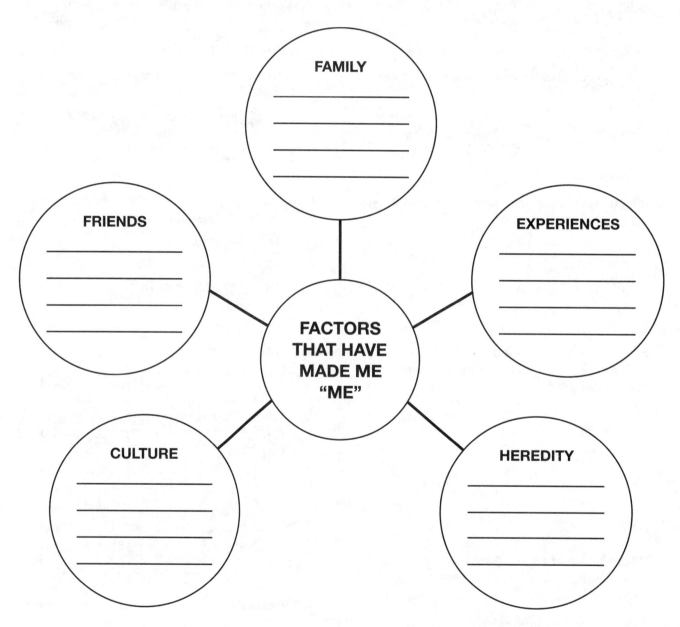

Social Studies

4.0

Cultural Influences on Personal Identity
Individual Development and Identity

DIRECTIONS: Choose the best answer.

1. **Omar prays five times every day while facing the city of Mecca. He studies a holy book called the *Quran*. Each year he celebrates a month-long holiday called *Ramadan*. Which religion does Omar practice?**

   (A) Christianity

   (B) Shintoism

   (C) Islam

   (D) Judaism

2. **In some countries, such as the United States and Italy, Christmas and Easter are important holidays. Most businesses are closed on these days. In other countries, such as Saudi Arabia and China, businesses are not closed on these holidays, which are not widely celebrated. What can we conclude from these facts?**

   (F) People in the United States and Italy are more religious than people in other countries.

   (G) No one should have to work on Christmas and Easter.

   (H) People in Saudi Arabia and China don't know how to have fun.

   (J) Christianity is widespread in the United States and Italy.

DIRECTIONS: Read the passage below, and then answer the questions that follow.

   For hundreds of years, young women in Latin America from Mexico to Argentina have celebrated their *quinceañera*—their 15th birthday—in grand tradition, beginning with a Catholic Mass and continuing on to a large and extravagant party. In some parts of the United States the tradition thrives, particularly among second- and third-generation Hispanic girls. *Quinceañera* parties are generally very lavish, with mariachi bands, a feast, and many guests celebrating the 15-year-old's transition into womanhood.

3. **In which of the following cities is a girl most likely to have a *quinceañera* party?**

   (A) New Delhi, India

   (B) Panama City, Panama

   (C) Paris, France

   (D) Vancouver, Canada

4. **A *quinceañera* party could be best described as a _____ .**

   (F) hazing

   (G) national holiday

   (H) wedding celebration

   (J) coming-of-age party

5. **On the lines below, name three groups to which you belong (for example: religious group, sports team, musician, sci-fi fan, American, gamer, etc.). For each group you name, list two things that you or others do that show you belong to this group.**

   _____

   _____

   _____

   _____

   _____

   _____

   _____

   _____

   _____

   _____

   _____

Name _____   Date _____

The Role of Schools in the United States

Individuals, Groups, and Institutions

DIRECTIONS: Read the chronology below and then answer the questions that follow.

Date	Event
1635	The first high school in the American colonies was started in Massachusetts.
1636	Harvard College, the first college in the American colonies, was started in Massachusetts.
1785	The first state university was chartered in Georgia.
1833	The first coeducational college (a college for both men and women) in the United States was started in Ohio.
1852	Massachusetts became the first state to pass a law requiring children to go to school.
1917	The Smith-Hughes Act provided federal money for vocational education.
1944	The GI Bill provided grants to veterans to continue their education.
1954	The Supreme Court ruled that public schools cannot be segregated, or separated by race.
1979	The U.S. Department of Education was established.

1. **In what year did the first high school in the colonies begin?**

   (A) 1635

   (B) 1636

   (C) 1785

   (D) 1833

2. **The chronology shows that _____ .**

   (F) education was not considered important in the United States before the 20th century

   (G) people in the United States have always had equal opportunities for education

   (H) schools have always been important institutions in the United States

   (J) The federal government is not interested in education

3. **What institution ruled that public schools could not be separated by race?**

   (A) Harvard College

   (B) the state of Massachusetts

   (C) the U.S. Supreme Court

   (D) the U.S. Department of Education

4. **Choose one of the events in the chronology and explain what group of people would have been most affected by that event.**

   _____

   _____

   _____

   _____

   _____

   _____

Name _____   Date _____

Social Studies

Changing Women's Rights
Individuals, Groups, and Institutions

DIRECTIONS: Read the passage below and then answer the questions that follow.

During the 1800s, many women in the United States began to work together for change. They worked for woman suffrage, or the right to vote, and were known as *suffragists*. The suffragists formed organizations to promote their cause. One such organization was the National Woman Suffrage Association. It was founded by Elizabeth Cady Stanton and Susan B. Anthony. This organization wanted an amendment to the Constitution that would allow women to vote in national elections. Another organization, the American Woman Suffrage Association, worked to allow women to vote in state elections. The two organizations combined in 1890 to form the National American Woman Suffrage Association. This organization was led by Anna Howard Shaw and Carrie Chapman Catt. By 1917, the organization had more than 2 million members.

The fight for woman suffrage was not easy, however. The suffrage movement created conflict. Many people did not like the idea of change and did not support giving women the right to vote. As a result, they formed groups to protest the idea. These groups said that giving women the right to vote would upset family life. They said it would lead to divorce and would result in children not being taken care of properly.

Nonetheless, the suffrage movement continued to gain more and more support. By 1913, several states had given women the right to vote. Finally, in 1919, Congress passed the Nineteenth Amendment, which gave women the right to vote, and in 1920 women participated for the first time in a presidential election.

1. **Who were the suffragists?**

   (A) people who worked to give women the right to vote

   (B) people who were against giving women the right to vote

   (C) politicians who passed the Nineteenth Amendment

   (D) politicians who opposed passing the Nineteenth Amendment

2. **Elizabeth Cady Stanton and Susan B. Anthony started _____ .**

   (F) the American Woman Suffrage Association

   (G) the National Woman Suffrage Association

   (H) the National American Woman Suffrage Association

   (J) groups to protest giving women the right to vote

3. **Which of the following is true?**

   (A) Everyone supported the suffrage movement.

   (B) The Nineteenth Amendment gave women the right to vote.

   (C) Women had the right to vote by 1848.

   (D) By 1913 there was still no support for the movement.

4. **In the space below, give two reasons that the suffrage movement caused conflict.**

   _____

   _____

   _____

   _____

   _____

Name _____   Date _____

Mini-Test 2

Individual Development and Identity;
Individuals, Groups, and Institutions

DIRECTIONS: For each of the following, give at least two examples and then explain what factors have influenced your choices.

1. **Activities you participate in:**

_____

_____

_____

Factors that have influenced your choice of activities:

_____

_____

_____

2. **Traditions you have:**

_____

_____

_____

Factors that have influenced the traditions you have:

_____

_____

_____

3. **Ways you dress:**

_____

_____

_____

Factors that influence how you dress:

_____

_____

_____

DIRECTIONS: Answer the following questions.

4. **What role have schools played in your life? Name at least two ways that schools have influenced you or made a difference in your life.**

_____

_____

_____

5. **List two groups or organizations that you are involved in (for example, sports teams, charity organizations, etc.). How does belonging to these groups or organizations help make you a unique individual?**

_____

_____

_____

_____

_____

Social Studies

6.0

The Political System
in the United States
Powers, Authority, and Governance

DIRECTIONS: Choose the best answer.

1. **Which of the following is not a function of government?**
   - (A) defending the country
   - (B) collecting taxes
   - (C) raising families
   - (D) educating citizens

2. **The United States has a form of government that allows its citizens to elect officials to represent them. This is best known as**

   _____ .
   - (F) federalism
   - (G) a dictatorship
   - (H) a monarchy
   - (J) a republic

3. **Which statement about elections in the United States is false?**
   - (A) Some judges are elected, and others are appointed.
   - (B) It is possible to vote for a Democratic president and Republican vice president.
   - (C) Voters can cast ballots for local officials, as well as for national officials.
   - (D) Sometimes voters have an opportunity to vote on important issues as well as on candidates.

4. **What branch of the United States government is responsible for making laws?**
   - (F) the judicial branch
   - (G) the executive branch
   - (H) the legislative branch
   - (J) the Supreme Court

5. **The Constitution provides for a system of checks and balances to keep any one branch of government from becoming too powerful. Which of the following shows the system of checks and balances at work?**
   - (A) The Supreme Court can veto a bill from Congress.
   - (B) The president can veto a bill that Congress passes.
   - (C) The president can say that a law is unconstitutional.
   - (D) The Senate can say that a law is unconstitutional.

6. **What is the role of the secretary of state in the United States government?**
   - (F) to carry out the nation's foreign policy
   - (G) to be responsible for the nation's law enforcement
   - (H) to care for the working conditions of the nation's workers
   - (J) to give advice for the ways schools are run

7. **The political system in the United States is based on federalism, which means that**

   _____ .
   - (A) the government is divided into three branches
   - (B) power is shared by the national government and the states
   - (C) each branch of government can check on the other branch
   - (D) the power to rule lies with the people

Name _____   Date _____

Purposes of Government and Protection of Individual Rights

Powers, Authority, and Governance

DIRECTIONS: Use the chart below to answer questions 1–4.

Purposes of Government

Purpose	Examples
To keep order	Passing laws and setting up courts
To provide security	Protecting citizens from enemies
To provide services	Providing clean water
To set public policy	Making decisions about the economy

1. **City governments pass laws to regulate traffic. What purpose of government does this illustrate?**

   (A) to set public policy

   (B) to provide services

   (C) to provide security

   (D) to keep order

2. **Which of the following is an example of government providing services?**

   (F) issuing food stamps to people who cannot afford to buy food

   (G) training soldiers in the military

   (H) ticketing drivers who run a red light

   (J) planning a budget

3. **Cutting taxes to help the economy is an example of government _____ .**

   (A) providing security

   (B) setting public policy

   (C) keeping order

   (D) providing services

4. **During World War II, the government drafted men to serve in the military. This is an example of what purpose of government?**

   (F) to set public policy

   (G) to provide services

   (H) to provide security

   (J) to keep order

DIRECTIONS: Choose the best answer.

5. **The right of newspapers to print views that differ from those of the government is an example of _____ .**

   (A) freedom of religion

   (B) freedom of speech

   (C) freedom of the press

   (D) freedom of assembly

6. **Which of the following is a way that people exercise their right to freedom of assembly?**

   (F) taking part in a demonstration against a government policy

   (G) a newspaper printing citizens' views in letters to the editor

   (H) being able to practice the religion of one's choice

   (J) giving one's opinion about an issue on a television show

7. **Police officers must have a warrant to search for evidence in the home of a person suspected of a crime. What individual right does this protect?**

   (A) the right to a speedy trial

   (B) protection against unreasonable searches

   (C) the right to freedom of assembly

   (D) protection against excessive punishment

Social Studies

Types of Economic Systems
Production, Distribution, and Consumption

DIRECTIONS: Choose the best answer.

1. **Suppose you want a new CD player. If you live in the United States, you would probably need to _____ .**

   (A) ask the government to give you one

   (B) go to the store and buy one

   (C) ask the government for permission, then go to the store and buy one

   (D) buy one from the government

2. **The kind of economic system where individuals own most of the stores, farms, and factories is called a _____ economy.**

   (F) socialist

   (G) command

   (H) market

   (J) developing

3. **The kind of economic system where the government controls most of the stores, farms, and factories is called a _____ economy.**

   (A) socialist

   (B) command

   (C) market

   (D) developing

4. **In a market economy, the price of a pound of hamburger _____ .**

   (F) never changes

   (G) rises a little bit every year

   (H) is set by the government

   (J) depends on how much hamburger is available and how many people want to buy it

5. **In the United States, who is allowed to buy a house?**

   (A) whoever the government allows to buy one

   (B) college graduates only

   (C) anyone who can afford to buy one

   (D) only top government officials

6. **Marcus manages an automobile factory. If he lives in a country that has a command economy, _____ .**

   (F) the government will probably tell him how many cars to build this month

   (G) he will decide all by himself how many cars to build this month

   (H) the employees of the factory will tell him how many cars they feel like making this month

   (J) he will probably examine sales figures before deciding how many cars to build this month

STOP

Social Studies

7.0 Specialization and Production
Production, Distribution, and Consumption

DIRECTIONS: Select the best answer.

1. When the production of a good is broken down into several separate tasks, with different workers performing each task, it is called _____ .

   Ⓐ productivity

   Ⓑ division of labor

   Ⓒ entrepreneurship

   Ⓓ unemployment

2. Building a car is a complicated job. The fastest way to build a car is _____ .

   Ⓕ for many people to do one part of the job and become very good at it

   Ⓖ for one person to build the car all alone

   Ⓗ both F and G would be equally fast

   Ⓙ F would be faster at first, but after a while G would be faster

DIRECTIONS: When workers are specialized, they have particular skills that they use to do their jobs. Specialization on the job has both good points and bad points. Write a **B** beside each condition if you think it is a benefit of specialization. Write a **D** if you think it is a disadvantage of specialization.

_____ 3. Over time, specialized workers become very good at what they do.

_____ 4. Production can slow down if a specialized worker is out sick.

_____ 5. Specialized workers make fewer mistakes.

_____ 6. Specialized workers may become bored performing the same task every day.

_____ 7. It takes less time to train a worker to do one or two tasks than to do many tasks.

8. At the Well-Built Bicycle Company, each bicycle is built completely by one person. At the Speedy Bicycle Company, a team of 15 specialized employees builds each bicycle. Each member of the team does a little bit of the work. Which company do you think builds more bicycles in a typical week? Explain your answer.

_____

_____

_____

_____

Name _____ Date _____

 8.0

Important Inventions
in Environmental History
Science, Technology, and Society

DIRECTIONS: Match the inventor in Column A with the invention in Column B. A clue is provided beside each inventor's name.

Column A

_____ 1. **Thomas Edison** *(bright idea)*

_____ 2. **James Watt** *(s-s-see it go!)*

_____ 3. **Alfred Nobel** *(boom boom)*

_____ 4. **Karl Benz** *(as in Mercedes)*

_____ 5. **William Siemens** *(hot stuff)*

_____ 6. **John Gorrie** *(he was cool)*

_____ 7. **John Deere** *(farm boy)*

Column B

A. **dynamite**

B. **early electric furnace**

C. **electric lightbulb**

D. **first mechanical refrigeration system**

E. **steam engine**

F. **early automobile**

G. **first steel plow**

8. **Explain the impact you think the electric lightbulb has had on the environment.**

_____

_____

_____

_____

_____

_____

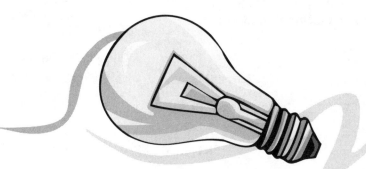

Social Studies

6.0–8.0

For pages 95–99

Mini-Test 3

Powers, Authority, and Governance; Production, Distribution, and Consumption; Science, Technology, and Society

DIRECTIONS: Choose the best answer.

1. **Which of the following is a way that the judicial branch checks the power of the legislative branch of government?**
   - (A) by vetoing bills
   - (B) by approving treaties
   - (C) by declaring laws unconstitutional
   - (D) by appointing judges

2. **Which government official's job involves making laws for the country?**
   - (F) a senator
   - (G) a governor
   - (H) the president
   - (J) Supreme Court justice

3. **A small city sends out snowplows to clean the streets after a snowstorm. What purpose of government does this illustrate?**
   - (A) to keep order
   - (B) to provide services
   - (C) to provide security
   - (D) to set public policy

4. **When people gather in Washington, D.C., to show their support for a cause, what right are they exercising?**
   - (F) freedom of religion
   - (G) freedom of the press
   - (H) freedom of assembly
   - (J) the right to vote

5. **In what kind of economic system are prices of goods determined by the government?**
   - (A) socialist
   - (B) market
   - (C) developing
   - (D) command

6. **In a factory producing bicycles, each worker performs a different aspect of the job. This is known as _____ .**
   - (F) command economy
   - (G) entrepreneurship
   - (H) division of labor
   - (J) market economy

7. **Which of the following is a benefit of specialization on a job?**
   - (A) knowing how to perform the work well
   - (B) not having skills to perform other kinds of jobs
   - (C) taking more time to train a worker
   - (D) becoming bored with the job

8. **Who invented dynamite?**
   - (F) Karl Benz
   - (G) Thomas Edison
   - (H) Alfred Nobel
   - (J) James Watt

STOP

Name _____   Date _____

Social Studies

International Organizations
Global Connections

DIRECTIONS: Use the information in the table to choose the best answer.

Name of Organization	Description
United Nations (UN)	Almost every country in the world is a member of the UN. Among its goals are to achieve higher standards of living, improve health and education, and promote respect for human rights and freedoms throughout the world. Its main objective, however, is to promote world peace.
Organization of American States (OAS)	Most nations in North and South America are members of the OAS. The goals of the OAS are to have peace and justice, to promote unity, and to defend the power, territory, and independence of each member nation.
Caribbean Community (CARICOM)	Fifteen Caribbean nations are members of CARICOM. The mission of CARICOM is to provide leadership and service to have a workable, internationally competitive community that can be maintained.
Andean Community	Bolivia, Colombia, Ecuador, Peru, and Venezuela make up the Andean Community. This organization promotes economic cooperation among its member nations.

1. **Which of the organizations cited in the table probably has the most member states?**

   (A) Andean Community

   (B) United Nations

   (C) Organization of American States

   (D) Caribbean Community

2. **Suppose Ecuador and Bolivia have a dispute concerning a trade agreement. Which of the following organizations would probably take the greatest interest in resolving the dispute?**

   (F) United Nations

   (G) Caribbean Community

   (H) Andean Community

   (J) Organization of American States

3. **Suppose two Central American countries were threatening to go to war against each other. Which of the following organizations would probably take a leading role in preventing the conflict?**

   (A) Organization of American States

   (B) Andean Community

   (C) Caribbean Community

   (D) both B and C but not A

4. **Which of the following organizations includes members outside of North America and Latin America?**

   (F) Andean Community

   (G) Organization of American States

   (H) United Nations

   (J) all of them include members outside of North America and Latin America

5. **The United States is not a member of the _____ .**

   (A) Andean Community

   (B) Caribbean Community

   (C) United Nations

   (D) both A and B but not C

Social Studies

9.0

The United States and Foreign Policy

Global Connections

DIRECTIONS: Choose the best answer.

1. **In which of the following ways does the United States become involved in the affairs of other nations?**
   - (A) providing money to help build schools
   - (B) sending food to countries unable to produce enough for their own people
   - (C) supplying military support
   - (D) all of the above

2. **In the United States, the _____ have the power to make treaties with foreign nations.**
   - (F) president and all 50 state governors
   - (G) president and the Senate
   - (H) mayors of the 25 largest American cities
   - (J) House of Representatives and the Supreme Court

3. **Which U.S. cabinet department is responsible for carrying out foreign policy?**
   - (A) Department of State
   - (B) Department of the Interior
   - (C) Department of Defense
   - (D) Department of Justice

4. **The term "foreign policy" means _____ .**
   - (F) the amount of money one nation sends to another
   - (G) the political policy of one nation in its relations with other nations
   - (H) one country wants to take over another country
   - (J) restricting the number of immigrants that come into a nation

5. **The United States has an official foreign policy regarding _____ .**
   - (A) Bolivia
   - (B) China
   - (C) Nigeria
   - (D) all of the above

6. **The United States sends officials called _____ to other nations. These are officials who usually live in the foreign nation and represent the United States in its dealings with the nation.**
   - (F) generals
   - (G) senators
   - (H) ambassadors
   - (J) attorneys

STOP

Name _____ Date _____

Social Studies

Political Ideals in the United States

Civic Ideals and Practices

DIRECTIONS: One of the most cherished ideals in America is that all people are created equal. Read the scenarios below and write a **C** in the space provided if you think it is consistent with this ideal. Write an **I** if you think it is inconsistent with this ideal.

_____ 1. **The practice of slavery**

_____ 2. **Women gain the right to vote**

_____ 3. **All accused criminals are entitled to legal representation**

_____ 4. **Charging a poll tax before allowing an individual to vote**

_____ 5. **Freedom of religion**

_____ 6. **Separate schools for white and black children are abolished**

DIRECTIONS: Read the passage and then answer the questions.

William was a U.S. citizen. William, however, did not like many things the president and Congress were doing. He thought their actions were wrong and immoral. So, William used his computer to make a booklet that told how much he disliked the U.S. government. He printed many copies of the booklet. Then, he went downtown and gave the booklets to people he passed on the street. He was not doing this in an angry way. If someone did not want the booklet, William simply moved on to the next person. He did not start any fights with anyone.

One woman did not like what William wrote in the booklet. She asked a police officer, who was patrolling nearby, to stop William from passing out his booklets. The police officer grabbed the box of booklets William was carrying and read one of them. Then, he took the booklets away from William and arrested him.

7. **Were any of William's constitutional rights violated in this incident?**

   Ⓐ No, William did not have the right to say bad things about the government.

   Ⓑ Yes, but William should have been arrested anyway because what he was doing was wrong.

   Ⓒ Yes, William's right to free speech was violated.

   Ⓓ Yes, William's right to freedom of religion was violated.

8. **William claimed that the police officer had no right to take his booklets away from him. Which constitutional right does William probably think the officer violated?**

   Ⓕ the thirteenth amendment, which made slavery illegal

   Ⓖ the fourth amendment, which limits the government's right to search or take personal belongings

   Ⓗ the third amendment, which prohibits the government from forcing citizens to house soldiers in their homes

   Ⓙ the second amendment, which gives citizens the right to own guns so that states can maintain militias

10.0 The Shaping of Public Policy
Civic Ideals and Practices

DIRECTIONS: Read the passage and answer questions 1 and 2.

In 1955, an African-American woman named Rosa Parks refused to give her seat on a city bus in Montgomery, Alabama, to a white passenger. At that time, her action was against the law. She was arrested. Many African Americans in Montgomery then boycotted, or refused to ride, city buses any longer. Two-thirds of city bus riders were African-American. As a result, the bus company lost most of its business. After more than a year, the law was changed and African Americans no longer had to give their seats to other bus passengers.

1. **In 1955, many African Americans in Montgomery, Alabama, _____ the city bus company.**
   - (A) lobbied
   - (B) boycotted
   - (C) petitioned
   - (D) banned

2. **How did the actions of the African-American community in Montgomery influence public policy?**
   - (F) An unfair, discriminatory law was changed.
   - (G) Bus fare for all riders was lowered.
   - (H) White bus riders had to give up their seats to African-American passengers.
   - (J) Public policy was not influenced by their actions.

DIRECTIONS: Choose the best answer.

3. **Special interest groups hire people to influence public officials for or against a specific cause. This person is called a _____ .**
   - (A) boycotter
   - (B) protester
   - (C) lobbyist
   - (D) candidate

4. **Which of the following is not a special interest group that tries to influence the way Congress votes on important issues?**
   - (F) National Rifle Association
   - (G) World Wildlife Federation
   - (H) National Organization for Women
   - (J) All of these groups try to influence the way Congress votes.

5. **Sometimes, individuals or groups do not like how the government or a company is handling something. They can show their disapproval by holding a demonstration. Some people demonstrate by picketing, or carrying signs that state their point of view. Some people demonstrate by sitting in front of a building of the company or government office with which they do not agree. This makes it difficult for other people to enter the building. People involved in these types of demonstrations are also called _____ .**
   - (A) petitioners
   - (B) protesters
   - (C) lobbyists
   - (D) candidates

Social Studies

| 9.0–10.0 |

For pages 101–104

Mini-Test 4

Global Connections; Civic Ideals and Practices

DIRECTIONS: Choose the best answer.

1. **Which of the following statements about the United Nations is true?**

   Ⓐ It is made up primarily of nations in North and South America.

   Ⓑ Its main purpose is to promote economic cooperation among its members.

   Ⓒ It is smaller than the Organization of American States but larger than the Andean Community.

   Ⓓ Its main objective is to promote world peace.

2. **A lobbyist is someone who _____ .**

   Ⓕ lives in a foreign nation and represents the United States in its dealings with that nation

   Ⓖ is hired by a special interest group to influence public officials for or against a specific cause

   Ⓗ takes part in a demonstration to show disapproval of how the government or a company is handling something

   Ⓙ refuses to buy a product or use a service as a method of protest

3. **Which of the following is not an acceptable way to influence public policy?**

   Ⓐ join a peaceful protest march

   Ⓑ threaten to stop buying a company's products if it continues practices you do not like

   Ⓒ offer to buy the mayor a new car if she votes the way you want her to on an important issue

   Ⓓ write a letter to the editor of the local newspaper expressing your opinion

4. **All Americans have a constitutional right to _____ .**

   Ⓕ three meals per day

   Ⓖ express their political opinions

   Ⓗ live in a nice house

   Ⓙ free health care

5. **The following table shows the five countries that received the most financial aid from the United States in 2000. What can we conclude from the table?**

Country	Amount of U.S. Foreign Aid Received in 2000
Israel	$4.069 billion
Egypt	$2.054 billion
Colombia	$0.902 billion
West Bank/Gaza	$0.485 billion
Jordan	$0.427 billion

   Ⓐ The U.S. government should stop spending money in other countries.

   Ⓑ The U.S. government is very interested in affairs in Israel and Egypt.

   Ⓒ The U.S. government does not help other countries.

   Ⓓ The U.S. government does not take good enough care of its own citizens.

6. **The United States stands for many ideals, such as freedom. Which of the following is an example of an inconsistency between what the United States is supposed to stand for and actual events?**

   Ⓕ allowing restaurants to refuse to serve people because of their race

   Ⓖ putting people in jail for acts of treason

   Ⓗ allowing people to say unpopular things

   Ⓙ stopping factories from polluting rivers and streams

How Am I Doing?

Mini-Test 1

Page 89

Number Correct

5 answers correct	**Great Job!** Move on to the section test on page 108.
4 answers correct	**You're almost there!** But you still need a little practice. Review practice pages 81–88 before moving on to the section test on page 108.
0–3 answers correct	**Oops!** Time to review what you have learned and try again. Review the practice section on pages 81–88. Then, retake the test on page 89. Now, move on to the section test on page 108.

Mini-Test 2

Page 94

Number Correct

5 answers correct	**Awesome!** Move on to the section test on page 108.
4 answers correct	**You're almost there!** But you still need a little practice. Review practice pages 90–93 before moving on to the section test on page 108.
0–3 answers correct	**Oops!** Time to review what you have learned and try again. Review the practice section on pages 90–93. Then, retake the test on page 94. Now, move on to the section test on page 108.

Mini-Test 3

Page 100

Number Correct

8 answers correct	**Great Job!** Move on to the section test on page 108.
5–7 answers correct	**You're almost there!** But you still need a little practice. Review practice pages 95–99 before moving on to the section test on page 108.
0–4 answers correct	**Oops!** Time to review what you have learned and try again. Review the practice section on pages 95–99. Then, retake the test on page 100. Now, move on to the section test on page 108.

How Am I Doing?

Mini-Test 4	6 answers correct	**Great Job!** Move on to the section test on page 108.
Page 105 **Number Correct**	4–5 answers correct	**You're almost there!** But you still need a little practice. Review practice pages 101–104 before moving on to the section test on page 108.
	0–3 answers correct	**Oops!** Time to review what you have learned and try again. Review the practice section on pages 101–104. Then, retake the test on page 105. Now, move on to the section test on page 108.

Final Social Studies Test
for pages 81–105

DIRECTIONS: Choose the best answer.

1. **As a citizen, you have a responsibility to take part in your community. All of the following are good ways to do this, except _____ .**

   (A) write to the president of a company protesting the treatment of women in the company's commercials

   (B) read the newspaper regularly

   (C) secretly remove books from the library that you think are unpatriotic

   (D) vote in every election

2. **Which of the following actions is unconstitutional?**

   (F) owning a hunting rifle

   (G) reading a book praising the September 11, 2001, attack on the United States

   (H) refusing to serve a customer in a bar because he has had too much to drink

   (J) refusing to serve a customer in a restaurant because she is Asian

3. **The Nineteenth Amendment did what?**

   (A) kept people from voting

   (B) repealed the Eighteenth Amendment

   (C) did away with slavery

   (D) gave women the right to vote

4. **The United States has this kind of economic system.**

   (F) socialist economy

   (G) developing economy

   (H) market economy

   (J) command economy

5. **Which of the following is a foreign policy issue for the U.S. government?**

   (A) China wants to tax all the vehicles it imports from the United States.

   (B) The state of Illinois wants to increase the gasoline tax by one cent.

   (C) Congress hopes to pass a new law that helps senior citizens in the U.S. get prescription drugs more easily.

   (D) You write a letter to your pen pal in Brazil.

6. **Which of the following is an aspect of culture?**

   (F) the way people meet their need for food and shelter

   (G) the ways people dress

   (H) the events people celebrate

   (J) all of the above

DIRECTIONS: Use the table below to answer question 7.

Desert	Tropical Rain Forest
Average temperature of 25°C	Average temperature of 25°C
Average annual rainfall of less than 25 cm	Average annual rainfall of more than 300 cm
Poor soil	Poor soil
Supports little plant life	Supports abundant plant life

7. **The physical environment of the desert _____ .**

   (A) guarantees that almost no farming will occur there

   (B) makes it impossible for people to live there

   (C) requires people to dress very warmly

   (D) supports more plant life than the environment in a rain forest

GO ➡

DIRECTIONS: Choose the best answer.

8. **Schools are an example of _____ .**

    (F) an important institution in the United States

    (G) how government provides security

    (H) the right to freedom of assembly

    (J) government foreign policy

9. **Who is the head of the executive branch of the U.S. government?**

    (A) the senator

    (B) the chief justice

    (C) the governor

    (D) the president

10. **The president can veto a bill that Congress passes, but Congress can override the veto. This is an example of _____ .**

    (F) federalism

    (G) separation of powers

    (H) the system of checks and balances

    (J) popular sovereignty

11. **Cities have sewer systems to dispose of waste. This is an example of government _____ .**

    (A) keeping order

    (B) providing security

    (C) providing services

    (D) setting public policy

12. **Thomas Edison invented _____ .**

    (F) dynamite

    (G) the electric lightbulb

    (H) the steam engine

    (J) the first steel plow

13. **Which of the following influences an individual's identity?**

    (A) family

    (B) friends

    (C) heredity

    (D) all of the above

14. **Specialization generally means that _____ .**

    (F) it takes more time to train a worker

    (G) a product can be produced more quickly

    (H) workers learn to do many tasks

    (J) workers have greater variety in their work

DIRECTIONS: Use the time line below to answer question 15.

Events Leading to the American Revolution			
Parliament passes the Stamp Act, which meets with the cry: "Taxation without representation!"	The Townshend Acts are passed.	The Boston Massacre occurs.	People protest during the Boston Tea Party.
1765	1767	1770	1773

15. **Which of these events happened first?**

    (A) Boston Tea Party

    (B) Townshend Acts

    (C) Boston Massacre

    (D) Stamp Act

GO →

Name _____ Date _____

DIRECTIONS: Use the map below to answer questions 16 and 17.

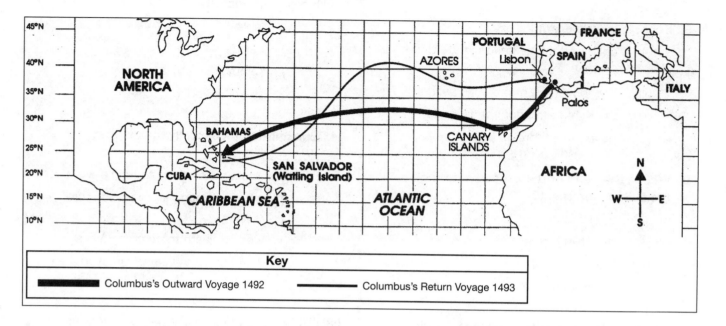

Key

─────── Columbus's Outward Voyage 1492   ─────── Columbus's Return Voyage 1493

16. **When Columbus sailed from Spain to the New World, in what direction did he travel?**

    (F)   due west

    (G)   southeast

    (H)   southwest

    (J)   northwest

17. **Which country did Columbus sail to upon his return?**

    (A)   Spain

    (B)   Portugal

    (C)   France

    (D)   Italy

DIRECTIONS: Choose the best answer.

18. **Peru is a member of all of the following organizations, except**

    (F)   the United Nations.

    (G)   the Organization of American States.

    (H)   the Caribbean Community.

    (J)   the Andean Community.

19. **Which of the following is a purpose of the United Nations?**

    (A)   to promote respect for human rights and freedoms throughout the world

    (B)   to establish laws within each member nation

    (C)   to provide food for all people in the world

    (D)   to train the military within each member nation

20. **In order to protect a person from unreasonable searches, the police must _____ before searching a person's home.**

    (F)   obtain a warrant

    (G)   pass a law

    (H)   have proof of a person's guilt

    (J)   have enough evidence to convict a person

Name _____ Date _____

Final Social Studies Test
Answer Sheet

1. (A) (B) (C) (D)
2. (F) (G) (H) (J)
3. (A) (B) (C) (D)
4. (F) (G) (H) (J)
5. (A) (B) (C) (D)
6. (F) (G) (H) (J)
7. (A) (B) (C) (D)
8. (F) (G) (H) (J)
9. (A) (B) (C) (D)
10. (F) (G) (H) (J)

11. (A) (B) (C) (D)
12. (F) (G) (H) (J)
13. (A) (B) (C) (D)
14. (F) (G) (H) (J)
15. (A) (B) (C) (D)
16. (F) (G) (H) (J)
17. (A) (B) (C) (D)
18. (F) (G) (H) (J)
19. (A) (B) (C) (D)
20. (F) (G) (H) (J)

Science Standards

Standard 1—Unifying Concepts and Processes *(See page 114.)*
As a result of the activities in grades K–12, all students should develop understanding and abilities aligned with the following concepts and processes:
- Systems, order, and organization.
- Evidence, models, and explanation.
- Constancy, change, and measurement.
- Evolution and equilibrium.
- Form and function.

Standard 2—Science as Inquiry *(See pages 115–116.)*
As a result of their activities in grades 5–8, all students should develop
- Abilities necessary to do scientific inquiry.
- Understandings about scientific inquiry.

Standard 3—Physical Science *(See pages 118–120.)*
As a result of their activities in grades 5–8, all students should develop an understanding of
- Properties and changes of properties in matter.
- Motion and forces.
- Transfer of energy.

Standard 4—Life Science *(See pages 121–124.)*
As a result of their activities in grades 5–8, all students should develop an understanding of
- Structure and function in living systems.
- Reproduction and heredity.
- Regulation and behavior.
- Populations and ecosystems.
- Diversity and adaptations of organisms.

Standard 5—Earth and Space Science *(See pages 125–126.)*
As a result of their activities in grades 5–8, all students should develop an understanding of
- Structure of the earth system.
- Earth's history.
- Earth in the solar system.

Standard 6—Science and Technology *(See page 128.)*
As a result of their activities in grades 5–8, all students should develop
- Abilities of technological design.
- Understandings about science and technology.

Standard 7—Science in Personal and Social Perspectives *(See page 129.)*
As a result of their activities in grades 5–8, all students should develop an understanding of
- Personal health.
- Populations, resources, and environments.
- Natural hazards.
- Risks and benefits.
- Science and technology in society.

Science Standards

Standard 8—History and Nature of Science *(See page 130.)*
As a result of their activities in grades 5–8, all students should develop an understanding of

- Science as a human endeavor.
- Nature of science.
- History of science.

Name Aida Qadeer   Date _____

Patterns of Change
Unifying Concepts and Processes

DIRECTIONS: Study the diagrams below and then answer the questions that follow.

Crescent Moon

Half Moon

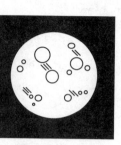
Full Moon

Half Moon

Crescent Moon

Winter

Spring

Summer

Fall

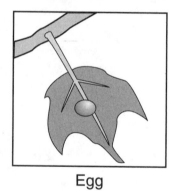
Egg

Larva

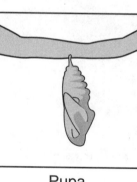
Pupa

Adult

1. **What do each of the diagrams above have in common?**

   They all have changes
   occuring in them.

2. **Why is it important to understand that changes occur in patterns?**

   So that we can better
   adapt to the changes
   around us.

3. **Think about the weather. If weather changes did not occur in predictable patterns, how might this change your daily life? Give examples.**

   You can't plan your
   day and activities ahead
   of time. For example,
   if you plan to go to
   the park, and it rains
   you can't go.

   STOP

Science

2.0

Formulating and Answering Questions
Science as Inquiry

DIRECTIONS: Read about Ryan's experiment and then answer the questions that follow.

Ryan wanted to find out if people could tell the difference between the taste of cold tap water and cold bottled water. He filled one glass pitcher with tap water and another glass pitcher with bottled water. Then, he placed the pitchers in the same refrigerator overnight.

1. What is the question that Ryan is trying to answer?

If people could tell the
difference between the
taste of cold tap water
and cold bottled wat-
_er._

2. What should be the next step in Ryan's experiment?

(A) He should ask several people to taste the tap water.

(B) He should ask several people to taste the bottled water.

● He should ask several people to taste both types of water and guess which one is tap water and which one is bottled water.

(D) He should ask several people to taste both types of water and tell which one they like the best.

3. After he has gathered the data, what should he do with it?

He should

4. How can Ryan best present his findings?

Ryan can best present
his findings on a

STOP

Science

2.0

The Practices of Science
Science as Inquiry

DIRECTIONS: Read the story below and then answer the questions that follow.

> Lauren entered the science fair. For her project, she wanted to see which brand of batteries lasts longest: Everglo, Glomore, or Everlasting. She decided to place new batteries into identical new flashlights, turn on the flashlights, then wait for the batteries to run down. She wrote down the following results: Everglo—lasted 19 hours; Glomore—lasted 17 hours; Everlasting—lasted 25 hours.
>
> She then decided to redo the experiment to confirm the results. For her second experiment, she placed new batteries into the old flashlights that her parents keep in the garage, the kitchen, and their bedroom. She then turned on the flashlights and waited for the batteries to run down. This time, she wrote down the following results: Everglo—lasted 13 hours; Glomore—lasted 16 hours; Everlasting—lasted 9 hours.
>
> Lauren was puzzled by the results of her second experiment. Because it was so similar to her first experiment, she thought she would get the same results.

1. **What is the best explanation for why Lauren's second experiment had different results than her first experiment?**

    (A) Lauren used different brands of batteries in the second experiment.

    (B) The second experiment used old flashlights, while the first experiment used new flashlights.

    (C) The second experiment was too much like the first experiment.

    (D) There is no good explanation; sometimes things just happen.

2. **How was Lauren sure that the results of the second experiment were different from the results of the first experiment?**

    (F) She read on the side of the battery packages how long each brand would last before it ran down.

    (G) She simply remembered how long it took each brand of battery to run down.

    (H) She recorded exactly how long it took each brand of battery to run down for each experiment.

    (J) She cannot be sure; her experiment was faulty.

3. **Tell what Lauren did right in her experiments. Could she have done anything in a better, more scientific way?**

    She recorded her experiments. To redo the experiments Lauren should have used the same type of flashlights she had used before. Or else, something different results would have occured.

4. **Which of these is an example of unsafe behavior in a science lab?**

    (A) wearing eye goggles

    (B) smelling and tasting unknown chemicals

    (C) avoiding the use of broken or chipped glassware

    (D) tying back long hair when working with flames

Mini-Test 1

Unifying Concepts and Processes; Science as Inquiry

DIRECTIONS: Read the stories below and then answer the questions that follow.

Lily and Corey lined one shoebox with white paper and another with black paper. Then, they put a thermometer in each shoebox. They placed both shoeboxes outside in the sun for one hour. At the start of the experiment, the temperature in both boxes was 72°F. At the end of the hour, the box with the white paper showed a temperature of 85°F, and the box with the black paper showed a temperature of 92°F. Two weeks later, they repeated the experiment with these differences: one shoebox was lined with yellow paper and another with orange paper. On that day, the sky was cloudy and the temperature in both boxes was 65°F at the beginning of the experiment.

1. **What will be the most likely outcome of the second experiment?**

   (A) The box with the yellow paper will show a temperature of 85°F, and the box with the orange paper will show a temperature of 92°F.

   (B) The box with the orange paper will show a temperature of 85°F, and the box with the yellow paper will show a temperature of 92°F.

   (C) Both boxes will show a temperature of 85°F.

   (D) The temperature inside the box with the orange paper will be a bit higher than the box with the yellow paper, but neither box will show temperatures as high as the boxes in the first experiment.

2. **Explain how you arrived at your answer to question 1.**

   Yellow and Orange are not as dark as black but brighter than white. Black absorbs energy and white reflects it. Yellow and Orange will get different temperature than white and black.

After discovering a moldy loaf of bread in a kitchen cabinet, Scott decided to do an experiment to determine the conditions under which mold grows the best. He suspected that mold grows best in the dark, so he put his idea to the test.

Scott bought a new loaf of bread and some sandwich bags. In each bag, he put a slice of bread, a damp paper towel, and a bit of soil. He put the bags in places that received different amounts of light, but would remain at room temperature.

In three days, Scott checked the bags. He found the most mold growing on the bread that he had put in a dark place.

3. **Which of the following best explains Scott's findings?**

   (F) Light affects the growth of mold.

   (G) Temperature does not affect the growth of mold.

   (H) Mold does not need water to grow.

   (J) The sandwich bags made the mold grow.

DIRECTIONS: Choose the best answer.

4. **Fatima went to the library. She looked up the average amount of rain that fell in Jacksonville, Florida, during the month of November for each of the last ten years. What can she predict with this information?**

   (A) She can predict about how much it will rain in Jacksonville, Florida, next April.

   (B) She can predict about how much it will rain in Chicago, Illinois, next November.

   (C) She can predict about how much it will rain in Jacksonville, Florida, next November.

   (D) She can predict about how much it will rain in Fort Meyers, Florida, next November.

Name _____ Date _____

Classifying Matter
Physical Science

DIRECTIONS: Choose the best answer.

Example:

If matter has a fixed volume, but changes its shape to fit its container, it is a ___liquid___ .

- (A) solid
- (B) liquid
- (C) gas
- (D) suspension

Answer: (B)

1. **How can you change matter from one state to another?**
   - (A) by changing its container
   - (B) by adding or removing heat
   - (C) by dividing it in half
   - (D) by changing its volume

2. **Ice is water in its ___Solid___ state.**
   - (F) solid
   - (G) changing
   - (H) liquid
   - (J) gas

3. **You fill a balloon with steam and then put it in the refrigerator. What do you predict will happen next?**
   - (A) The balloon will expand.
   - (B) The balloon will contract.
   - (C) The balloon will pop.
   - (D) The balloon will not change.

4. **When water freezes, it changes from a ___liquid to solid___**
   - (F) gas to a solid
   - (G) liquid to a gas
   - (H) liquid to a solid
   - (J) solid to a gas

5. **If matter expands to fill the volume of its container, it is a ___gas___ .**
   - (A) solid
   - (B) liquid
   - (C) gas
   - (D) suspension

6. **Which of the following cannot be used to classify forms of matter?**
   - (F) water
   - (G) liquid
   - (H) gas
   - (J) solid

STOP

Science
3.0

Variables and Properties
Physical Science

DIRECTIONS: Choose the best answer.

1. A diamond is able to cut glass due to its _____ .

   (A) mass

   (B) hardness

   (C) elasticity

   (D) texture

2. Sound travels faster in steel than in water because the particles of matter in steel _____ .

   (F) vibrate faster

   (G) are farther apart

   (H) are closer together

   (J) vibrate more slowly

3. Magdalena has dropped a box of antique needles in a haystack. Some of the needles are made of wood, some are made of iron, and some are made of bone. If she runs a magnet over the haystack, which needles will she be able to find?

   (A) wooden needles

   (B) iron needles

   (C) bone needles

   (D) none of the needles

4. Which property describes why you are able to blow bubbles with chewing gum?

   (F) texture

   (G) elasticity

   (H) magnetism

   (J) hardness

5. You are investigating objects that float. Which of the following properties would describe an object most likely to float?

   (A) hardest

   (B) softest

   (C) greatest mass

   (D) least mass

6. Which of the following could you use to conduct electricity?

   (F) metal wire

   (G) tree branch

   (H) plastic drinking straw

   (J) none of the above

7. Jeannie filled one beaker with 100 mL of cold water. She filled another beaker with 100 mL of hot water and added red food coloring to make it red. She then used an eyedropper to put drops of the hot, red water into the beaker of cold water. The drops of red water floated to the top, and the red water made a layer on top of the layer of cold water in the beaker. Jeannie can conclude from her experiment that _____ .

   (A) hot water is more dense than cold water

   (B) hot water is less dense than cold water

   (C) hot water and cold water have the same density

   (D) neither hot nor cold water have any density

Science

3.0

Forces
Physical Science

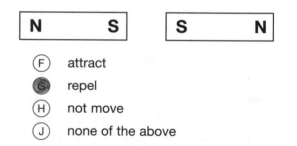

DIRECTIONS: Choose the best answer.

1. The force that pulls a skydiver back to earth is called _____ .
   - (A) gravity
   - (B) mass
   - (C) friction
   - (D) inertia

2. A man standing at the top of the Grand Canyon accidentally knocked some pebbles over the edge. What force will cause them to fall?
   - (F) gravity
   - (G) magnetism
   - (H) friction
   - (J) solar power

3. Slippery Sam pours salad oil on the floor because he likes watching people slip when they step on it. Before asking him to oil all the door hinges as punishment, Sam's teacher asks him to explain why oil makes people slip and keeps door hinges from squeaking. If Sam answers correctly, he will say that oil cuts down on _____ .
   - (A) gravity
   - (B) inertia
   - (C) friction
   - (D) mass

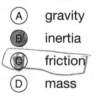

4. If a marble and a baseball are both dropped 10 feet from the ground at the same time, what will happen?
   - (F) The marble will hit the ground first.
   - (G) The baseball will hit the ground first.
   - (H) The marble and the baseball will hit the ground at the same time.
   - (J) none of the above

5. Dot decided to go home and ride in her wagon. She asked her brother Jorge to push her. At first, he pushed her very gently. After a while, he pushed harder. Then, Sandra came to visit, and Jorge pushed both of them in the wagon at the same time. Which of the following is true?
   - (A) Dot went slower when Jorge pushed harder. Dot and Sandra had more gravity than just Dot.
   - (B) Dot went faster when Jorge pushed harder. Dot and Sandra were harder to move than just Dot.
   - (C) Dot went slower when Jorge pushed harder. Dot and Sandra were easier to move than just Dot.
   - (D) Dot went faster when Jorge pushed harder. Dot and Sandra were easier to move than just Dot.

6. What will happen between these two magnets?

N	S		S	N

   - (F) attract
   - (G) repel
   - (H) not move
   - (J) none of the above

STOP

Science

[4.0]

Relationships Among Organisms
Life Science

DIRECTIONS: Choose the correct word from the parentheses at the end of each sentence to fill in the blanks and complete the definitions.

1. The place where an organism lives is

   its ___habitat___ .
   (habitat, community)

2. All of the living organisms within an area form

   a ___community___ .
   (community, habitat)

3. The unique role of an organism in the community is

   its ___habitat___ .
   (habitat, niche)
   ___niche___

4. A biological community and physical environment that interact to form a stable system is called

   a(n) ___ecosystem___ .
   (ecosystem, niche)

5. An organism, usually a green plant, which can make its own food is called

   a ___prducer___ .
   (consumer, producer)

6. An organism that lives by feeding on other organisms is called

   a ___consumer___ .
   (decomposer, consumer)

7. An organism that feeds on the remains of other organisms is called

   a ___decomposer___ .
   (decomposer, producer)

DIRECTIONS: Answer questions 8 and 9 based on the food chain shown below.

8. Which of the following statements is true?

   Ⓐ   Mice eat foxes.

   Ⓑ   Snakes eat mice.

   Ⓒ   Nothing in this food web eats snakes.

   Ⓓ   Owls eat deer.

9. What would be the most likely result in this ecosystem if all the foxes were removed?

   Ⓕ   The eagles would begin eating deer.

   Ⓖ   The plants would all die.

   Ⓗ   The deer population would increase.

   Ⓙ   The owls, snakes, and eagles would have more mice to eat.

STOP

Name _____   Date _____

Science

Classification of Organisms
Life Science

DIRECTIONS: Choose the best answer.

1. Animals that have backbones are called
   _____ .
   - (A) carnivores
   - (B) herbivores
   - (C) vertebrates
   - (D) invertebrates

2. Which of the following is an invertebrate?
   - (F) frog
   - (G) monkey
   - (H) worm
   - (J) bird

3. Animals that usually have the same body
   temperature regardless of whether their
   surroundings are warm or cold are called
   _____ .
   - (A) cold-blooded
   - (B) warm-blooded
   - (C) terrestrial
   - (D) aquatic

4. Fish breathe using _____ .
   - (F) lungs
   - (G) gills
   - (H) scales
   - (J) fins

5. Which of the following vertebrates is cold-
   blooded but has lungs?
   - (A) fish
   - (B) birds
   - (C) mammals
   - (D) reptiles

6. Animals that spend part of their lives in water
   and part on land are called _____ .
   - (F) fish
   - (G) amphibians
   - (H) reptiles
   - (J) mammals

7. Birds and many insects have _____ to
   help them travel and escape predators.
   - (A) teeth
   - (B) stingers
   - (C) fins
   - (D) wings

8. Animals whose babies drink their mother's
   milk are called _____ .
   - (F) birds
   - (G) fish
   - (H) mammals
   - (J) reptiles

9. One difference between a lion cub and a
   flower seedling is that only the _____ .
   - (A) lion cub needs food
   - (B) flower seedling needs water
   - (C) lion cub can move from place to place
   - (D) flower seedling has parents

10. How do plants get their food?
    - (F) They get it from outside themselves.
    - (G) They create it using photosynthesis.
    - (H) They get it during pollination.
    - (J) Plants do not need food.

11. Plants that produce flowers and fruits are
    _____ .
    - (A) angiosperms
    - (B) gymnosperms
    - (C) conifers
    - (D) lycopsids

12. Which of the following is an example of
    a gymnosperm?
    - (F) a tomato plant
    - (G) a wildflower
    - (H) an apple tree
    - (J) a fir tree

STOP

Name _____ Date _____

Plant and Animal Cells
Life Science

DIRECTIONS: Read the passage below, and then answer the questions that follow.

Cells of Living Things

Cells are the smallest and most basic units of living matter. They are the small pieces that when put together make organs, plants, and even people. All living things are made of cells, though not all cells are exactly alike.

Both animal and plant cells have a cell membrane, which holds all the cell parts together. The nucleus is one of the largest parts of the cell. It is the command center of the cell and controls the activities in the cell. Chromosomes inside this command center control what an organism will be like. For instance, your chromosomes carry the information that makes you have blue or brown eyes and black or red hair. Cytoplasm is the thick liquid that all the parts of the cell float in. It's mostly water, but also has some important chemicals inside.

Both plant and animal cells have mitochondria. These are where food is burned to give the cell energy. Animal and plant cells also have some differences. The plant cell has a cell wall, just outside the cell membrane, that makes the cell stiff. Both animal and plant cells have vacuoles, but animals have far more and they are much smaller. Finally, plant cells have chloroplasts. These are where the cell produces chlorophyll. This chemical makes food for the plant when the sunlight hits it. This is how a plant feeds itself.

Plants and animals are multicelled organisms. Cells that make up multicelled organisms are specialized. Unlike single-celled organisms, such as bacteria, specialized cells found in larger organisms cannot survive outside of the organism. Single-celled organisms carry out all life activities. But specialized cells work as a team to meet the life activities of every cell inside a multicelled organism.

1. **Which part of a cell is the command center?**
   - (A) membrane
   - (B) nucleus
   - (C) cytoplasm
   - (D) mitochondria

2. **In what part of the cell is food burned to give the cell energy?**
   - (F) membrane
   - (G) nucleus
   - (H) cytoplasm
   - (J) mitochondria

3. **What two parts does a plant cell have that an animal cell does not have?**
   - (A) cell wall and chloroplasts
   - (B) membrane and cytoplasm
   - (C) nucleus and cytoplasm
   - (D) nucleus and mitochondria

4. **Which of the following is true of single-celled organisms?**
   - (F) Their cells are specialized.
   - (G) Their cells carry out all life activities.
   - (H) They cannot survive alone.
   - (J) They work as a team with other cells.

Name _____ Date _____

DIRECTIONS: Use the passage on the previous page to help you fill in the labels of the missing cell part names.

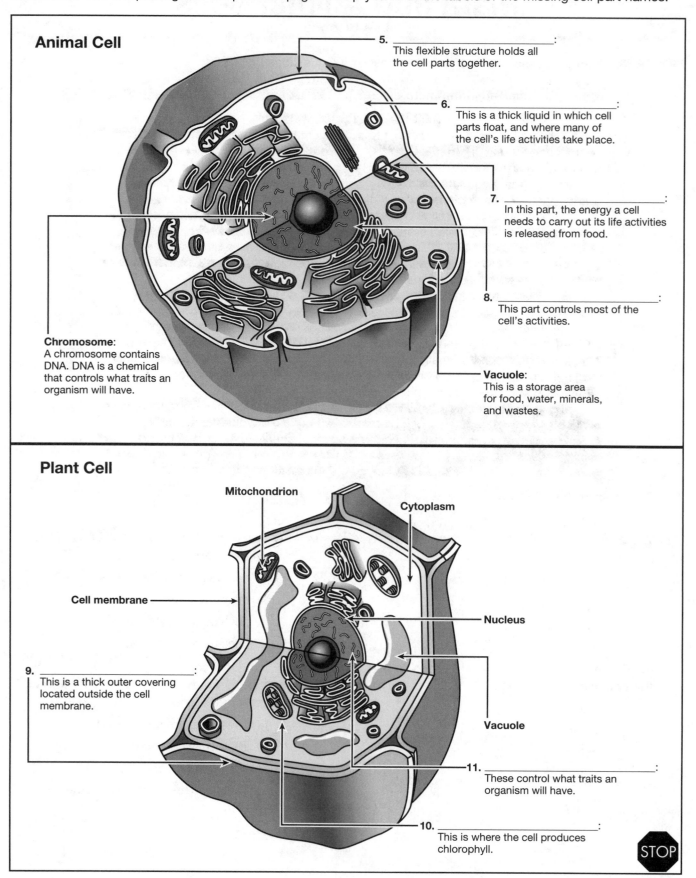

Animal Cell

5. _____:
This flexible structure holds all
the cell parts together.

6. _____:
This is a thick liquid in which cell
parts float, and where many of
the cell's life activities take place.

7. _____:
In this part, the energy a cell
needs to carry out its life activities
is released from food.

8. _____:
This part controls most of the
cell's activities.

Chromosome:
A chromosome contains
DNA. DNA is a chemical
that controls what traits an
organism will have.

Vacuole:
This is a storage area
for food, water, minerals,
and wastes.

Plant Cell

Mitochondrion

Cytoplasm

Cell membrane

Nucleus

9. _____:
This is a thick outer covering
located outside the cell
membrane.

Vacuole

11. _____:
These control what traits an
organism will have.

10. _____:
This is where the cell produces
chlorophyll.

STOP

Science
5.0

Earth's Processes
Earth and Space Science

DIRECTIONS: Choose the best answer.

1. **The changes that occurred in the pictures below are probably due to _____ .**

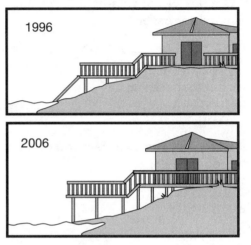

1996

2006

- (A) pollution
- (B) erosion
- (C) tornadoes
- (D) condensation

2. **Christopher was looking at pictures of different mountain ranges in the United States. He was surprised to see that the Appalachian Mountains were smaller and more rounded than the Rocky Mountains. The Appalachian Mountains looked old and worn compared to the Rocky Mountains.**

- (F) The effect of wind and water caused erosion, wearing away the mountains.
- (G) Too many people and animals traveled across the mountains, causing them to wear away.
- (H) All of the snowfall was so heavy that it weighted down the mountains and caused them to shrink.
- (J) The water that used to cover Earth wore away parts of the mountains.

3. **During the Ice Age, most of the state of Illinois was covered by a huge glacier that changed the landscape. Which of the following was not an effect of the glacier on the landscape of that state?**

- (A) New mountains were made.
- (B) The peaks of hills were scraped off.
- (C) Many deep valleys were filled in.
- (D) Soil was transported miles away from its origin.

4. **What kind of mountains are the Hawaiian Islands?**

- (F) fault-block
- (G) volcanic
- (H) upwarped
- (J) folded

5. **The Adirondack Mountains are upwarped mountains. Today, the rock material that was once present on the tops of these mountains is gone. Why?**

- (A) The rock material was pushed inside earth.
- (B) Sharp peaks and ridges formed over the rock material.
- (C) The rock material became magma.
- (D) The rock material was eroded.

6. **Which of the following is the slowest type of mass movement?**

- (F) abrasion
- (G) creep
- (H) slump
- (J) mudflow

GO

7. Which term describes a mass of snow and ice in motion?

(A) loess deposit

(B) glacier

(C) outwash

(D) abrasion

8. Which characteristic is common to all agents of erosion?

(F) They carry sediments when they have enough energy of motion.

(G) They are most likely to erode when sediments are moist.

(H) They create deposits called *dunes*.

(J) They erode large sediments before they erode small ones.

9. When a puddle of water disappears after the sun comes out, it is called _____ .

(A) displacement

(B) metamorphosis

(C) isolation

(D) evaporation

10. Water vapor forming droplets that form clouds directly involves which process?

(F) condensation

(G) respiration

(H) evaporation

(J) transpiration

11. Most of Earth's water is in _____ .

(A) glaciers

(B) lakes

(C) streams

(D) the oceans

12. All the water that is found on Earth's surface is the _____ .

(F) carbosphere

(G) hydrosphere

(H) precipitation

(J) pollution

13. 97 percent of the water on Earth is _____ .

(A) salt water

(B) freshwater

(C) rainwater

(D) fog

14. What is a mixture of weathered rock and organic matter called?

(F) soil

(G) limestone

(H) carbon dioxide

(J) clay

15. What is another term for decayed organic matter found in soil?

(A) leaching

(B) humus

(C) soil

(D) sediment

16. What occurs when weathered rock and organic matter are mixed together?

(F) leaching

(G) oxidation

(H) soil erosion

(J) soil formation

17. In the water cycle, how is water returned to the atmosphere?

(A) evaporation

(B) condensation

(C) precipitation

(D) fixation

18. Warm, low-pressure air can hold more water than cold air. As warm air rises, it cools. This causes water vapor to gather together, or condense, into water drops. What kind of weather probably goes along with low air pressure?

(F) clouds and rain

(G) clouds without rain

(H) clear skies

(J) tornadoes

Science

| 3.0–5.0 |

Mini-Test 2

For pages 118–126   **Physical Science; Life Science; Earth and Space Science**

DIRECTIONS: Choose the best answer.

1. **Malcolm left a cube of ice in a glass on a windowsill. In about an hour, the ice changed into a clear substance that took on the shape of the lower part of the glass. Finally, after three days, there appeared to be nothing in the glass at all. Which states of matter did the ice cube pass through?**

   Ⓐ liquid then gas then solid

   Ⓑ solid then liquid then gas

   Ⓒ gas then liquid then solid

   Ⓓ solid then gas then liquid

2. **Baseball pitchers use several forces to change the motion of the ball. One force is the strong push from the pitcher's arm that starts the ball moving toward home plate. Which force pulls the ball down as it moves?**

   Ⓕ velocity

   Ⓖ friction

   Ⓗ inertia

   Ⓙ gravity

3. **The force that acts against the movement of two touching surfaces is _____ .**

   Ⓐ friction

   Ⓑ heat

   Ⓒ motion

   Ⓓ velocity

4. **Why would a nail be attracted to a magnet?**

   Ⓕ It is made of steel or iron.

   Ⓖ It weighs less than the magnet.

   Ⓗ It is thinner than the magnet.

   Ⓙ all of the above

5. **Which of the following is an example of a vertebrate animal?**

   Ⓐ fly

   Ⓑ worm

   Ⓒ bird

   Ⓓ starfish

6. **Animal cells have _____ .**

   Ⓕ cell walls

   Ⓖ chloroplasts

   Ⓗ cytoplasm

   Ⓙ large vacuoles

7. **A pear tree is an example of _____ .**

   Ⓐ an angiosperm

   Ⓑ a gymnosperm

   Ⓒ a fern

   Ⓓ a lycopsid

8. **Which part of plant and animal cells contains chromosomes?**

   Ⓕ nucleus

   Ⓖ cytoplasm

   Ⓗ membrane

   Ⓙ vacuole

9. **Which two forces cause erosion?**

   Ⓐ water and gravity

   Ⓑ sun and wind

   Ⓒ wind and water

   Ⓓ gravity and wind

10. **A producer is an organism that _____ .**

   Ⓕ can make its own food

   Ⓖ feeds on other organisms

   Ⓗ feeds on the remains of other organisms

   Ⓙ is at the top of the food chain

Science

| 6.0 |

Effects and Influence
of Technology
Science and Technology

DIRECTIONS: Match the need on the right with an example of how humans have used technology to meet that need. Some needs may be used more than once.

_____ 1. development of hunting tools

_____ 2. building fires

_____ 3. invention of cars

_____ 4. development of written language

_____ 5. building of forts

_____ 6. invention of the printing press

_____ 7. irrigation

_____ 8. development of antibiotics

_____ 9. invention of the jet engine

_____ 10. invention of the transistor radio

_____ 11. development of coal mining technology

Needs

A. warmth

B. food

C. shelter

D. communication

E. transportation

F. health

12. **How do you think the invention of computers has influenced society? How has it influenced you and other people in your family? Give some specific examples.**

_____

_____

_____

_____

_____

_____

13. **Name at least one technological innovation that you think has had an overall bad influence on society. Explain why you think it has had a bad influence.**

_____

_____

_____

_____

_____

_____

STOP

Science

| 7.0 |

Identifying Inherited Traits
Science in Personal and Social Perspectives

DIRECTIONS: For each of the following, put an **I** in the blank if it is an inherited trait. Leave all others blank.

1. _____ riding a bike

2. _____ hair color

3. _____ the number of petals on a flower

4. _____ hibernation

5. _____ counting

6. _____ eye color

7. _____ talking

8. _____ direction a tree grows

9. _____ curly or straight tails in pigs

10. _____ bees building hives

11. _____ dogs shaking hands

12. _____ birds laying eggs

13. Height is a trait that is inherited, but can be affected by the environment. Give some examples of environmental factors that may affect how tall a person becomes.

_____

_____

_____

_____

_____

_____

_____

_____

_____

_____

_____

_____

_____

_____

_____

STOP

Selected Scientific Achievements

History and Nature of Science

DIRECTIONS: Use the chronology of scientific achievements below to answer the questions.

Date	Event
c. 400 B.C.	Hippocrates, a Greek physician, teaches that diseases have natural causes.
c. A.D. 100s	Ptolemy, a Greek astronomer and geographer teaches that Earth is the center of the universe.
1543	Nicolaus Copernicus, a Polish astronomer, proposes idea that the sun is the center of the universe.
1628	William Harvey, an English physician, discovers how blood circulates in human beings.
Mid-1600s	Robert Hooke, an English scientist, discovers plant cells by using a microscope.
Mid-1700s	Carolus Linnaeus, a Swedish botanist, begins the scientific classification of plants and animals.
1830s	Theodor Schwann, a German physiologist, proves that all organisms are made up of cells.
Mid-1800s	Louis Pasteur, a French microbiologist, discovers that some bacteria cause diseases.

1. **How were the theories of Ptolemy and Copernicus different?**

_____

_____

_____

2. **How might the work of Hooke have influenced the work of Schwann?**

_____

_____

_____

3. **Identify three scientists whose work laid the foundation for modern medicine.**

_____

_____

_____

Science

6.0–8.0

For pages 128–130

Science and Technology; Science in Personal and Social Perspectives; History and Nature of Science

DIRECTIONS: Choose the best answer.

1. **Which of the following is an inherited ability?**

   Ⓐ tying shoes

   Ⓑ blinking

   Ⓒ skating

   Ⓓ reading

2. **Which of the following is a learned trait?**

   Ⓕ cheek dimples

   Ⓖ shape of ears

   Ⓗ language

   Ⓙ skin color

3. **Which scientific achievement contributed most to the study of medicine?**

   Ⓐ Andreas Vesalius writes the first scientific book on the human body in 1543.

   Ⓑ Joseph Priestly discovers oxygen in the 1770s.

   Ⓒ Johannes Kepler establishes astronomy as a science.

   Ⓓ Robert Boyle uses experimentation in the study of chemistry in the mid-1600s.

4. **Which need did the invention of the telephone meet?**

   Ⓕ warmth

   Ⓖ shelter

   Ⓗ transportation

   Ⓙ communication

5. **Describe one way a scientist might use technology to communicate the findings of an experiment to other scientists.**

   _____

   _____

   _____

   _____

   _____

6. **Describe one way technology has made it easier for scientists to help people stay healthy.**

   _____

   _____

   _____

   _____

   _____

STOP

How Am I Doing?

Mini-Test 1 Page 117 **Number Correct**	**4** answers correct	**Great Job!** Move on to the section test on page 133.
	3 answers correct	**You're almost there!** But you still need a little practice. Review practice pages 114–116 before moving on to the section test on page 133.
	0–2 answers correct	**Oops!** Time to review what you have learned and try again. Review the practice section on pages 114–116. Then, retake the test on page 117. Now, move on to the section test on page 133.
Mini-Test 2 Page 127 **Number Correct**	**9–10** answers correct	**Awesome!** Move on to the section test on page 133.
	5–8 answers correct	**You're almost there!** But you still need a little practice. Review practice pages 118–126 before moving on to the section test on page 133.
	0–4 answers correct	**Oops!** Time to review what you have learned and try again. Review the practice section on pages 118–126. Then, retake the test on page 127. Now, move on to the section test on page 133.
Mini-Test 3 Page 131 **Number Correct**	**6** answers correct	**Great Job!** Move on to the section test on page 133.
	4–5 answers correct	**You're almost there!** But you still need a little practice. Review practice pages 128–130 before moving on to the section test on page 133.
	0–3 answers correct	**Oops!** Time to review what you have learned and try again. Review the practice section on pages 128–130. Then, retake the test on page 131. Now, move on to the section test on page 133.

Final Science Test
for pages 112–131

DIRECTIONS: Use the information from the graph below to answer questions 1 and 2.

Anthony did an experiment to see how the flight of a paper airplane would be affected by changing the angle of the airplane's wings. He constructed three paper airplanes, slanting the wings down on Plane 1, and slanting them up on Plane 2. The wings of Plane 3 were level.

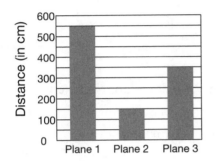

1. **Anthony might have decided to make a graph because it made it easier to _____ .**
   - (A) keep his data organized
   - (B) compare the distances each plane flew
   - (C) draw conclusions about his data
   - (D) all of the above

2. **Which of the following conclusions can Anthony draw from the graph?**
   - (F) Paper airplanes fly best with their wings pointed up.
   - (G) Paper airplanes fly best with level wings.
   - (H) Paper airplanes fly best with their wings pointed down.
   - (J) Real airplanes fly best with level wings.

DIRECTIONS: Choose the best answer.

3. **When water melts from an ice cube, this is an example of a physical change. The water changes from a _____ .**
   - (A) solid to a gas
   - (B) liquid to a vapor
   - (C) solid to a liquid
   - (D) liquid to solid

4. **On Tuesday afternoon, there was a summer shower in Dallas. The next day, Josh noticed the water puddle on the sidewalk in front of his house was becoming smaller and smaller. Which of the following explains what happened to the water?**
   - (F) It was absorbed by the sidewalk.
   - (G) It turned into a gas.
   - (H) It melted.
   - (J) It froze.

5. **Study the table below. Predict which season the southern hemisphere will have during the month of September.**

Month	Northern Hemisphere	Southern Hemisphere
December	Winter	Summer
March	Spring	Fall
June	Summer	Winter
September	Fall	?

   - (A) fall
   - (B) winter
   - (C) summer
   - (D) spring

6. **When water enters a crack in a rock and then freezes, what will possibly happen to the rock?**
   - (F) The crack might get larger and split the rock.
   - (G) The rock might become stronger due to the ice.
   - (H) The rock might melt and change into an igneous rock.
   - (J) none of these

GO

7. Which animal is highest in the food chain?

   (A) insect

   (B) snake

   (C) rat

   (D) bear

8. Which animal would be lowest in a food chain?

   (F) frog

   (G) mosquito

   (H) duck

   (J) man

9. Look at the food chain. Which missing animal might fit in the space?

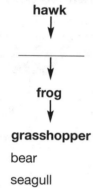

hawk

↓

_____

↓

frog

↓

grasshopper

   (A) bear

   (B) seagull

   (C) snake

   (D) elephant

10. Johann showed a rock to his Aunt Gordy, a geologist. She said that it looked as though it had been in a river or stream for a long time. Which of the following is most likely true?

   (F) The rock contains stripes of lots of colors.

   (G) The rock contains very old fossils.

   (H) The rock is rough with very sharp edges.

   (J) The rock is smooth with rounded edges.

11. Which of the following animals are warm-blooded?

   (A) fish

   (B) mammals

   (C) amphibians

   (D) reptiles

12. Chromosomes are found in the _____ of a cell.

   (F) membrane

   (G) cytoplasm

   (H) nucleus

   (J) mitochondria

13. A tomato plant is an example of _____ .

   (A) an angiosperm

   (B) a gymnosperm

   (C) a fern

   (D) a lycopsid

14. Which is not part of the water cycle?

   (F) evaporation

   (G) condensation

   (H) precipitation

   (J) respiration

15. Which of the following is not true about glaciers?

   (A) Most of Earth's water is in the form of glaciers.

   (B) Melting glaciers supply water for many people.

   (C) Glacial movements can fill in valleys.

   (D) Glaciers pick up boulders and sediment as they move.

GO

16. Which of the following statements about plants is not true?

(F) Plant cells have chlorophyll.

(G) Plants get food from outside themselves.

(H) Plants have limited movement.

(J) Plants have the ability to reproduce.

17. Study the table below. Which month is likely to have the most hurricanes?

Table of Tropical Storms and Hurricanes (1886–1996)		
Month Formed	Tropical Storms	Hurricanes
January–April	4	1
May	14	3
June	57	23
July	68	35
August	221	?
September	311	?
October	188	?
November	42	22
December	6	3

(A) July

(B) August

(C) September

(D) October

18. Which of the following is an inherited trait?

(F) eye color

(G) hair color

(H) skin color

(J) all of the above

19. Which of the following is a learned characteristic?

(A) shoe size

(B) height

(C) the ability to read

(D) all of the above

20. Darion is boiling some soup in a pot. He notices that when he takes the lid off the pot, drops of water are clinging to the inside of the lid. The lid was dry when he first put it on the pot. How did the water get from the pot to the inside of the lid?

(F) It froze there and melted.

(G) It melted and evaporated.

(H) It evaporated and condensed.

(J) It melted and evaporated.

21. Which word best describes the type of materials that attract iron?

(A) magnetic

(B) chemical

(C) mass

(D) physical

22. What will happen between these two magnets?

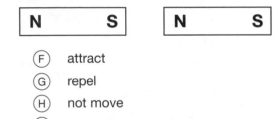

| N | S | N | S |

(F) attract

(G) repel

(H) not move

(J) none of these

23. Which of these is a conductor of electricity?

(A) rubber

(B) metal

(C) plastic

(D) wood

24. The development of the World Wide Web is a way that people have used technology to meet their need for _____ .

(F) shelter

(G) transportation

(H) communication

(J) health

Name _____   Date _____

Final Science Test
Answer Sheet

1 Ⓐ Ⓑ Ⓒ Ⓓ
2 Ⓕ Ⓖ Ⓗ Ⓙ
3 Ⓐ Ⓑ Ⓒ Ⓓ
4 Ⓕ Ⓖ Ⓗ Ⓙ
5 Ⓐ Ⓑ Ⓒ Ⓓ
6 Ⓕ Ⓖ Ⓗ Ⓙ
7 Ⓐ Ⓑ Ⓒ Ⓓ
8 Ⓕ Ⓖ Ⓗ Ⓙ
9 Ⓐ Ⓑ Ⓒ Ⓓ
10 Ⓕ Ⓖ Ⓗ Ⓙ

11 Ⓐ Ⓑ Ⓒ Ⓓ
12 Ⓕ Ⓖ Ⓗ Ⓙ
13 Ⓐ Ⓑ Ⓒ Ⓓ
14 Ⓕ Ⓖ Ⓗ Ⓙ
15 Ⓐ Ⓑ Ⓒ Ⓓ
16 Ⓕ Ⓖ Ⓗ Ⓙ
17 Ⓐ Ⓑ Ⓒ Ⓓ
18 Ⓕ Ⓖ Ⓗ Ⓙ
19 Ⓐ Ⓑ Ⓒ Ⓓ
20 Ⓕ Ⓖ Ⓗ Ⓙ

21 Ⓐ Ⓑ Ⓒ Ⓓ
22 Ⓕ Ⓖ Ⓗ Ⓙ
23 Ⓐ Ⓑ Ⓒ Ⓓ
24 Ⓕ Ⓖ Ⓗ Ⓙ

Answer Key

Page 9

Hibernation Includes facts

Main purpose is to inform

Organized according to the purpose the authors wish to achieve (steps to achieve a goal; explain why something happens; attempt to make an argument; etc.)

Waterland Made up or fantasized

Main purpose is to entertain

Organized into setting, characters, problem, goal, events, and resolution

Page 10

1. passages A, B, C, and E
2. passage F
3. passage B
4. passage C
5. passage A

Pages 11–12

1. A
2. The lines in the passage all rhyme.
3. A. squirrel, adoring
   B. rabbit, practical
4. Answers will vary. One possible answer is the value of knowing where you belong.
5. myth
6. science fiction
7. realistic fiction
8. nonfiction

Page 13

1. textbook
2. newspaper
3. biography
4. instruction manual
5. A
6. G

Page 14

1. First passage—journal; Second passage—newspaper article
2. Ben Hanson wrote the first passage; the second passage appeared in the newspaper.
3. Answers will vary. Possible answers: Both passages tell that (a) Ben missed the word *cannibal;* (b) a girl named Rebecca won the spelling bee; and (c) Ben won a dictionary.
4. Answers will vary. Possible answers: (a) only the diary entry tells how nervous Ben was at first; (b) only the newspaper entry tells Rebecca's last name; (c) only the newspaper article tells how many words Ben spelled correctly.

Page 15

1. what you spend your money on
2. items you subtract from your income
3. items you add to your income
4. relationship between debits and credits; the amount you have available to spend

Page 16

1. B
2. F
3. B
4. J
5. C
6. J

Page 17
Mini-Test 1

1. C
2. G
3. C
4. J
5. B
6. F
7. C
8. H

Pages 18–19

1. week
2. sale
3. meet
4. blew
5. Answers will vary but may include *beautiful, attractive, good-looking.*
6. Answers will vary but may include *burning, scorching, boiling.*
7. Answers will vary but may include *ugly, homely, unattractive.*
8. Answers will vary but may include *cold, chilly, freezing.*
9. A
10. H
11. B
12. F
13. C
14. G
15. D
16. F
17. C
18. J
19. B
20. H
21. A
22. G

Page 20

1. IN
   You are on a deserted island: no town, no people—just you and those crazy, noisy seagulls. What are you going to do?
2. none
   Toward the castle she fled. She begged the gatekeeper for entrance. He was as deaf as a gargoyle. He did not hear her cries. Past the stone walls she scurried, the hounds in pursuit.
3. none
   Maggie bit her lip. No use crying about it. She pulled her math homework out of the sink and just stared at her little sister.
4. IN
   The music is playing those lovely Christmas tunes, but you're not listening. You can't. You have too many important things to plan. What should you buy for Teddie? Who should you invite

to the party?
And . . .

5. none

   I'm not proud of it. Really, I am not. But no teacher's ever gotten through to me. I guess I'm just not cut out to be a scholar.

6. EX

   Columbus stood on the deck of the ship. Land was on the horizon. Land! Not the edge of the world, not dragons to devour the ship, but the land that would make his fortune . . . his and Spain's.

7. EX

   I think Mama forgot me. Otherwise, she would come and find me. Oh, no! I've been bad! Mama said not to go see the toys because I'd get lost. Mama is going to be mad at me!

8. IM

   Do not stop until you reach the end of this story. What you are about to read is so amazing that you simply must hear about it now. So settle back and get ready for the most incredible tale you've ever heard.

9.–10. Answers will vary. Students should include all four sentence types at least once in the paragraphs.

Page 21
1. C
2. I can ride faster than you can. Let's race to the stop sign.
3. I'm thirsty. Does anyone have some bottled water?
4. We need to be careful on the bike trail. In-line skaters can appear fast.
5. C
6. I love the playground. It has great swings.
7. When I swing too high, I get sick. Do you?
8. C
9. This ride was fun. Let's do it again tomorrow.
10.–13. Students' answers will vary but they should correctly rewrite each fragment into a complete sentence.

Page 22
1. Answers will vary but should include three memorable experiences.
2. Answers will vary but should describe the students' chosen experiences.
3. Answers will vary but should describe the three most important things the students would want to relate about their chosen experiences.

Page 23
1. B
2. J
3. C
4. G

Page 24
1. D
2. G
3. C
4. F
5. D

Page 25
1. B
2. H
3. A
4. J
5. B
6. F
7. led
8. where
9. due
10. it's
11. there
12. here
13. you're
14. read
15. sent

Pages 26–27
1. laid
2. laid
3. laid
4. lie
5. except
6. affect
7. accepted
8. except
9. D
10. J
11. A
12. H
13. D
14. J
15. B
16. J
17. D
18. G
19. D
20. G
21. B
22. F
23. A
24. F
25. D
26. G
27. C

Page 28
1. B
2. H
3. B
4. J
5. D
6. F

Page 29
Mini-Test 2
1. A
2. J
3. B
4. G
5. C
6. G
7. D
8. Answers will vary. Students should write about their favorite desserts and should include at least one interrogative and one exclamatory sentence in their paragraphs.

Page 30
Answers will vary. Students are to find a print and a nonprint source on a topic of their choice, describe each, and tell the main idea and supporting evidence found in each. Students should then compare information found in each source.

Pages 31–32
1. C
2. Possible answers include *bendable, limber, movable*.
3. Possible answers include *rigid*.
4. Possible answers include *relaxing on one's back; lying flat.*

5. book, encyclopedia article, magazine article
6. the encyclopedia article
7. volume 12
8. pages 25–32
9. the book
10. H
11. A
12. G
13. D
14. G
15. C

Page 33
Mini-Test 3
1. B
2. G
3. C
4. J
5. A
6. J

Page 34
1. why the sun and moon appear in the sky
2. why porcupines have four claws on each foot
3. One Who Walks All Over the Sky and Walking About Early; Porcupine and Beaver
4. They both cared about their environment and wanted to change it.

Page 35
Answers will vary. In the first paragraph, students should choose three things that need improvement in their community. In the second paragraph, students should give reasons why these things should be improved. In the concluding paragraph, students should explain what they could personally do to make these improvements.

Page 36
Answers will vary, but students' paragraphs should explain an activity using a logical order of directions and sufficient detail.

Page 37
Mini-Test 4
Student's paragraph should describe his or her favorite way to spend a day. Student should provide plenty of details and words that express his or her feelings.

Pages 40–42 Final English Language Arts Test
1. D
2. J
3. B
4. F
5. A
6. J
7. A
8. G
9. B
10. J
11. C
12. H
13. A
14. F
15. B
16. F
17. C
18. J
19. D
20. G

Page 45
1. >
2. <
3. >
4. =
5. >
6. =
7. >
8. =
9. >
10. >
11. =
12. <
13. D
14. G
15. A
16. J

Page 46
1. C
2. G
3. porpoise: −2
bird: 4
eel: −9
flag on sailboat: 3
sea horse: −7
octopus: −4
clouds: 6
jellyfish: −6
4. Circled items: porpoise, clouds, flag, sail of boat, buoy, bird
5. eel, jellyfish, octopus, porpoise, buoy, bird, clouds

Page 47
1. C
2. F
3. C
4. J
5. B
6. H

Page 48
1. $2 \times 6 + 2 \times 3$
$2 \times 9 = 12 + 6$
$18 = 18$
2. $(3 \times 4) + (3 \times 3)$
$21 = (4 + 3)3$
$21 = 21$
3. $(4 \times 9) - (4 \times 1)$
$4 \times 8 = 36 - 4$
$32 = 32$
4. $(9 \times 2) - (3 \times 2)$
$12 = (9 - 3)2$
$12 = 12$
5. $2 \times 15 - 2 \times 3$
$12 \times 2 = 30 - 6$
$24 = 24$
6. $(7 \times 8) + (5 \times 8)$
$12 \times 8 = 56 + 40$
$96 = 96$
7. $(5 \times 5) - (3 \times 5)$
$10 = (5 - 3)5$
$10 = 10$
8. $(3 \times 5) + (3 \times 6)$
$3 \times 11 = 15 + 18$
$33 = 33$
9. $(2 \times 4) + (3 \times 4)$
$20 = 8 + 12$
$20 = 20$

Page 49
1. D
2. F
3. D
4. F
5. C
6. G
7. C
8. J
9. A
10. H

Page 50
1. A
2. F
3. C
4. J
5. B
6. G

Page 51
1. C
2. J
3. D
4. G
5. A
6. J

Page 52
1. A
2. H
3. B
4. H
5. B
6. G
7. C

Page 53
1. 5th—15;
   6th—21;
   7th—28;
   8th—36
2. The pattern grows by successive integers: +2, +3, +4, +5, +6, etc.
3. 55
4. 5th—12;
   6th—14;
   7th—16;
   8th—18
5. The number of guests increases by two for each table added.
6. 22

Page 54
Mini-Test 1
1. C
2. F
3. B
4. H
5. D
6. G
7. A

Page 55
1. pentagon
2. decagon
3. triangle
4. pentagon
5. dodecagon
6. hexagon
7. octagon
8. quadrilateral (parallelogram)
9. D
10. F
11. B
12. A
13. C
14. E

Page 56
1. prism
2. neither
3. pyramid
4. pyramid
5. prism
6. neither
7. prism
8. pyramid
9. prism

Page 57
1. F = (2,6),
   L = (5,6),
   A = (5,4),
   G = (5,2)
2. B = (−2,2),
   O = (1,2),
   X = (1,−1),
   D = (−2,−1)
3. S = (2,−3),
   H = (2,−5),
   A = (−2,−5),
   P = (−2,−6),
   E = (−5,−6)
4. C

Page 58
1. congruent
2. congruent
3. congruent
4. similar
5. congruent
6. similar
7. D
8. J

Page 59
1. Triangle
2. Rectangle
3. Scalene triangle
4. Square
5. Pyramid
6. Sphere

Page 60
1. A
2. G
3. D

Page 61
1. 400 mm
2. yes
3. 250 cm
4. yes
5. B
6. J
7. 3 L
8. 40 L
9. 6,000 L
10. 1,000 daL
11. 250 daL
12. .7L
13. 8 kL
14. 10,000 g
15. 10 dag
16. 2 kg

17. .5 kg
18. 7 kg
19. 2,000 mg
20. 3,000 kg

Page 62
1. 13 centimeters
2. 1.25 inches
3. .25 mile
4. 4 meters
5. 20,000 feet
6. C
7. F
8. C
9. F
10. A
11. G

Page 63
1. 5
2. 6
3. 6
4. 5
5. 16

Page 64
1. B
2. H
3. A
4. 9
5. 9
6. 9

Page 65
Mini-Test 2
1. A
2. G
3. B
4. G
5. D
6. F
7. C

Page 66
1. 10
2. Number of People
3. 67
4. The vertical axis should be labeled: 0, 10, 20, 30, 40, 50, 60, 70, 80, 90, 100. The bars on the bar graph should reflect the numbers shown in the chart.

5. Answers will vary. Possible answer: Had Gina asked diners at an Italian restaurant about their favorite place to eat, she would probably have received more than 85 votes for Italian because people who are eating at an Italian restaurant probably enjoy Italian food.

Page 67
1. Last Year: 31 items
   This Year: 43 items
2. 12 items
3. greatest increase: canned goods; decrease: infant clothing
4. There was more variation this year. The difference between the low and high amounts collected per item (the range) was 31. Last year, it was 21.
5. Based on this set of data, the class can predict that next year's collection will increase slightly over this year's collection.

Page 68
1. D
2. G
3. B
4. F
5. C
6. H

Page 69
1. A
2. F
3. B
4. H
5. 0
6. NA
7. 1

Page 70
1. C
2. J
3. B
4. H
5. D
6. F
7. C

Page 71
1. D
2. J
3. C
4. G
5. C
6. G

Page 72
1. B
2. F
3. D
4. G
5. C
6. J

Page 73
1. A
2. J
3. A
4. H
5. B

Page 74
Mini-Test 3
1. A
2. J
3. B
4. H
5. B
6. H

Pages 76–78 Final Mathematics Test
1. B
2. F
3. B
4. J
5. D

6. H
7. D
8. H
9. B
10. J
11. C
12. G
13. D
14. G
15. A
16. G
17. C
18. F
19. C
20. H
21. A
22. J
23. A

Page 81
1. C
2. J
3. A
4. H

Page 82
1. A
2. H
3. B
4. G
5. A
6. H
7. D

Pages 83–84
1. B
2. H
3. Answers will vary, but students may base their own arguments on those of Samuel Johnson.
4. Answers will vary but should be supported with logical arguments.

Page 85
1. 1994; it allowed listeners to hear sounds almost at the moment they were said.
2. after
3. Eisenhower sets up an agency for technology.

4. A computer network is planned.
5. 8
6. 50 million

Page 86
1. B
2. G
3. A
4. J
5. D
6. H

Page 87
1. D
2. F
3. C
4. F
5. Answers will vary. One possible answer: People build their homes on high stilts to avoid the regularly occurring floodwaters.
6. Answers will vary. One possible answer: (1) Excessive heat and (2) inadequate rainfall could put a farmer's crop in jeopardy.

Page 88
1. C
2. F
3. D
4. J
5. C

Page 89
Mini-Test 1
1. D
2. F
3. A
4. J
5. D

Page 90
Students' responses will vary, but students should indicate how family, heredity, culture, friends, and experiences have

contributed to making them unique individuals.

Page 91
1. C
2. J
3. B
4. J
5. Answers will vary, but students should name three groups and give two examples that show they belong to each group.

Page 92
1. A
2. H
3. C
4. Answers will vary, but students should explain why that group would be most affected by the event in the chronology.

Page 93
1. A
2. G
3. B
4. Answers may include any two of the following: People did not like change; they thought giving women the right to vote would upset family life; they believed it would lead to divorce and neglect of children.

Page 94
Mini-Test 2
1–3. Answers will vary. Students should list their activities, traditions, and ways of dress and explain what factors have influenced them.

4. Answers will vary, but students should name two ways schools have influenced them.
5. Answers will vary. Students should indicate the groups or organizations they are involved in and explain how their participation contributes to making them unique individuals.

Page 95
1. C
2. J
3. B
4. H
5. B
6. F
7. B

Page 96
1. D
2. F
3. B
4. H
5. C
6. F
7. B

Page 97
1. B
2. H
3. B
4. J
5. C
6. F

Page 98
1. B
2. F
3. B
4. D
5. B
6. D
7. B

8. The Speedy Bicycle Company probably builds more bicycles in a typical week. Specialization and division of labor usually increase productivity of workers.

Page 99
1. C
2. E
3. A
4. F
5. B
6. D
7. G
8. Answers will vary. Students should explain how they think the electric lightbulb has impacted the environment.

Page 100
Mini-Test 3
1. C
2. F
3. B
4. H
5. D
6. H
7. A
8. H

Page 101
1. B
2. H
3. A
4. H
5. D

Page 102
1. D
2. G
3. A
4. G
5. D
6. H

Page 103
1. I
2. C
3. C
4. I
5. C
6. C
7. C
8. G

Page 104
1. B
2. F
3. C
4. J
5. B

Page 105
Mini-Test 4
1. D
2. G
3. C
4. G
5. B
6. F

Pages 108–110 Final Social Studies Test
1. C
2. J
3. D
4. H
5. A
6. J
7. A
8. F
9. D
10. H
11. C
12. G
13. D
14. G
15. D
16. H
17. B
18. H
19. A
20. F

Page 114
1. Each shows a pattern related to the natural world.
2. to help understand and predict future events
3. Answers will vary. Students should note that planning outdoor events would be nearly impossible if weather patterns were not somewhat predictable.

Page 115
1. Can people tell the difference between cold tap water and cold bottled water?
2. C
3. Ryan needs to analyze the data he collected and then draw conclusions from the data. He should decide if the conclusions support his original hypothesis.
4. Answers will vary. Students might suggest that Ryan present his findings in graph form along with his written report.

Page 116
1. B
2. H
3. Answers may vary. Possible answer: Lauren made accurate, detailed records of the results of her experiment. However, she

should have either used new flashlights for both experiments, or used the same old flashlights for both experiments. This would have given her a better idea of how long the batteries last under specific conditions.

4. B

Page 117
Mini-Test 1
1. D
2. Answers will vary. One possible answer is that the day of the second experiment is cooler than the day of the first experiment, so the temperature is not likely to rise to the same level as it did on the day of the first experiment. Nevertheless, yellow is a light color like white, and orange is a darker color like black; the darker, orange box is likely to be warmer than the lighter, yellow box, based on the results of the first experiment.
3. F
4. C

Page 118
1. B
2. F
3. B
4. H
5. C
6. F

Page 119
1. B
2. H
3. B
4. G
5. D
6. F
7. B

Page 120
1. A
2. F
3. C
4. H
5. B
6. G

Page 121
1. habitat
2. community
3. niche
4. ecosystem
5. producer
6. consumer
7. decomposer
8. B
9. J

Page 122
1. C
2. H
3. B
4. G
5. D
6. G
7. D
8. H
9. C
10. G
11. A
12. J

Pages 123–124
1. B
2. J
3. A
4. G
5. Cell membrane
6. Cytoplasm
7. Mitochondrion
8. Nucleus
9. Cell wall
10. Chloroplast
11. Chromosomes

Pages 125–126
1. B
2. F
3. A
4. G
5. D
6. G
7. B
8. F
9. D
10. F
11. D
12. G
13. A
14. F
15. B
16. J
17. A
18. F

Page 127
Mini-Test 2
1. B
2. J
3. A
4. F
5. C
6. H
7. A
8. F
9. C
10. F

Page 128
1. B
2. A
3. E
4. D
5. C
6. D
7. B
8. F
9. E
10. D
11. A
12. Answers will vary. One possible answer: Computers have allowed more work to be done at a faster rate than would otherwise have been possible.

Computers allow family members to stay in closer touch with one another.
13. Answers will vary. One possible answer: Excessive television viewing has resulted in a more sedentary population, damaging the overall health of the population.

Page 129
1. (blank)
2. I
3. I
4. I
5. (blank)
6. I
7. (blank)
8. (blank)
9. I
10. I
11. (blank)
12. I
13. Answers will vary. Students may note that factors such as nutrition may affect height.

Page 130
1. Ptolemy believed that Earth was the center of the universe, whereas Copernicus believed that the sun was the center.
2. Answers may vary, but students might indicate that Hooke discovered plant cells and Schwann built on Hooke's work by proving that all organisms are made of cells.
3. Hippocrates, Harvey, and Pasteur

Page 131
Mini-Test 3
1. B
2. H
3. A
4. J
5. Answers will vary. Possible answer: A scientist may communicate findings to other scientists by e-mail.
6. Answers will vary. Possible answer: Heart monitors have allowed doctors to keep better track of their patients' conditions.

Pages 133–135
Final Science Test
1. D
2. H
3. C
4. G
5. D
6. F
7. D
8. G
9. C
10. J
11. B
12. H
13. A
14. J
15. A
16. G
17. C
18. J
19. C
20. H
21. A
22. F
23. B
24. H